# NOTES
## *ON THE*
# PIANO

*Ernst Bacon*

✱

New Introduction by
Sara Davis Buechner

Dover Publications, Inc.
Mineola, New York

*To*

# FRANK PISKOR

*Copyright*

Copyright © 1963 by Syracuse University Press.
Introduction copyright © 2011 by Sara Davis Buechner.
All rights reserved.

*Bibliographical Note*

This Dover edition, first published in 2011, is an unabridged republication of
the work originally published by Syracuse University Press in 1963. A new
Introduction has been specially prepared by Sara Davis Buechner.

*Library of Congress Cataloging-in-Publication Data*

Bacon, Ernst, 1898–1990.
    Notes on the piano / Ernst Bacon; with a new introduction by Sara Davis
Buechner.
        p. cm.
    "This Dover edition, first published in 2011, is an unabridged republica-
tion of the work originally published by Syracuse University Press in 1963."
    ISBN-13: 978-0-486-48366-5
    ISBN-10: 0-486-48366-5
    1. Music—Quotations, maxims, etc. 2. Piano—Instruction and study. I.
Buechner, Sara Davis, 1959- II. Title.

ML66.B23 2011
786.2—dc23

                                                                2011017589

Manufactured in the United States by Courier Corporation
48366502
www.doverpublications.com

# Introduction to the Dover Edition

*"The Artist should not forget his mission, perhaps*
*the most religious of all, of sustaining faith in the*
*worthwhileness of art and thus of life."*
                                    —Ernst Bacon

The present volume found its way into the hands of this reader while still a teenage conservatory undergraduate, and rapidly became one of the most treasured books on my piano shelf. Although *Notes on the Piano* is ostensibly Ernst Bacon's contribution to the pedagogic literature about classical piano playing, it is as unlike a book about daily scales and pedalling insights as, say, the philosopher Krishnamurti's meditations are unlike a self-help stress relief primer. Bacon's open-ended approach to the vast literature, technique, interpretation and very *ethos* of the piano, its music and its connection to the creative heart, leads his lucky reader to a position not so much of conclusion, but to a renewed starting place of wide-eyed, continual learning, questioning, and discovery.

Ernst Bacon was born in Chicago on May 26, 1898, and showed early gifts in the manifold fields of music, art, poetry and mathematics. Early studies at Northwestern University and the Universities of Chicago and California were followed by two years of work in Europe. His teachers included Ernest Bloch for composition, Alexander Raab and Glenn Dillard Dunn for piano, and Eugene Goosens for conducting. Upon his return from Europe in the mid-1920s, Bacon began to make his name in many fields. He founded the Carmel Bach Festival in 1935, served as supervising conductor of the San Francisco Federal Music Project, and later became Dean of the School of Music at Converse College in Spartanburg, South Carolina, a position he held until 1945. For the next twenty years he made Syracuse University his base of operations, working there in succession as Professor of Piano and Director of the School of Music, and later as Composer-in-Residence. Upon his retirement in 1964, Bacon returned to his beloved California coast and continued to compose, virtually until the day he died on March 16, 1990 at the age of 91 in the town of Orinda, near Berkeley.

It was as a profoundly American composer that Bacon was most known during his lifetime, forging a proudly nationalistic path alongside his contemporaries Aaron Copland (b. 1900) and Roy Harris (b. 1898). Winner of the 1932 Pulitzer Prize in Composition for his Second Symphony and recipient of three Guggenheim Fellowships, he wrote copiously for orchestra, chamber ensemble, and piano—*Riolama* (1963) for piano and orchestra, and two important folk operas in collaboration with Paul Horgan: *A Tree on the Plains* (1942) and *Ford's Theater* (1946). American literature was perhaps dearest to Bacon's heart, and it was in his numerous operas, oratorios, cantatas and especially song cycles—set to the poetry of Emily Dickinson, William Blake, Walt Whitman, Carl Sandburg, and other American masters—that he combined his loves of melody, literature, and profoundly nationalistic spirit. Somewhat along the lines of the Hungarian Béla Bartók, he collected folk music of the American heartland. Appalachian songs, Southern spirituals, patriotic melodies, and cowboy tunes all figured in his original music and transcriptions, which he included in his own piano anthologies *Along Unpaved Roads: Songs of a Lonesome People, Byways,* and *Maple Sugaring*, as well as in collations of pedagogic children's pieces.

Bacon's cosmopolitan thirst and Renaissance nature led him to comradeship with the poet Carl Sandburg, African-American lyric tenor Roland Hayes, playwright Thornton Wilder, journalists Herb Caen and H. L. Mencken, and countless other leading American cultural figures. But the most significant of his artistic friendships was with the environmentalist photographer Ansel Adams (1902–1984). Their shared love of music was buttressed by a profound respect for nature and enthusiasm for mountaineering. Soon after Adams' passing in 1985, Bacon memorialized his friend in the moving elegy for solo clarinet, timpani, and string orchestra, *Remembering Ansel Adams* (1985).

***

Ernst Bacon's output as a writer was, if necessarily smaller than his work as a composer, scarcely less distinguished in quality. At the tender age of 19 he wrote his musical treatise, *Our Musical Idiom* (1917) in which he explored some of the new harmonies of the post-tonal age. While at Converse College he served as music critic for its weekly newspaper, *The Argonaut,* and he remained an avid contributor to magazines and University reviews throughout his life. In addition to his later volumes, *Notes on the Piano* (1963) and *Words on Music* (1966) he left many unpublished manuscripts and poems upon his death.

The magic of *Notes on the Piano* lies in its unique and enchanting presentation of the material. As Bacon states at the outset, "this is a book to be nibbled … its thought is not successive nor cumulative. Its last chapter could as well be its first." The book takes the form of statements, phrases, aphorisms, and short essays. The overall format presents itself in five parts, loosely arranged according to a subjective subdivision of the pianist's musical rôles—as student, performer, listener, and commentator. Some of the observations of one chapter overlap with another. But any preliminary assumption by the reader that Bacon's essays are wholly improvisatory is mistaken, and one can imagine a twinkle in the author's eye as he wrote that opening pithy salvo, clearly meant as a come-on to the reader to dive in. Although it is true that the book can be delightfully sampled, dipped into as with a ladle into a punchbowl of refreshing iced Sangria, it is perhaps best savored slowly through the voyage from first page to last.

There is indeed method to Bacon's thoughts, and the pattern of subject matter leads the reader on a rewarding journey that is not unlike the discoveries a pianist makes in learning a new work of, say, Beethoven or Schumann. The opening three chapters pose many of the questions often faced by an interpreter upon digesting a new musical score. How to proceed? What is the correct tempo? What's this melody all about? Then, in the next trio of chapters one is plunged into the "Musical Woodshed" (otherwise known to pianists as the Practice Room). Now it's time for the nitty-gritty: technical questions of which fingers to use, how to hold the arms, control of contrapuntal lines, understanding the composer's style. In one fascinating and particularly useful section, Bacon opines on the concept of how equality of fingerwork can be effected by the practice of symmetrical mirror scales, a keyboard technique particularly beloved of 20th-century composers Vincent Persichetti (a friend of Bacon's) and Einojuhani Rautavaara.

Upon exiting frying pan that is the practice room, pianists traditionally enter the fire of the piano lesson, and thus in the third section of *Notes on the Piano,* where Bacon leads his readers into the world of musical education, teaching and learning, and the larger academic sphere. Moreover, from this point forward, Bacon's book truly blooms into larger and larger ruminations upon the art of musical performance, the message of the artist, the obligations of the performer, and the meaning of music itself. In Chapters xi and xiii are the author's most poetic effusions. Not surprisingly, it is in this part of the book that Ernst Bacon draws most clearly upon his apparently boundless cultural resources. His ability to make metaphorical connections between music and the other arts seems limitless. A quick mention of just a few of the cultural titans cited in these chapters—Shakespeare, Rembrandt, Bach, Goethe, Beethoven, Mendelssohn, Manet, Liszt, Henry James, Whistler, Strauss, Eakins, Cassatt, Monet, Edward MacDowell, Diego Rivera, Ernest Bloch, Griffes, Theodore Dreiser, Jack London—gives a mere glint of the astonishing cosmopolitan erudition of Ernst Bacon.

With the air of a satisfied master host, Bacon completes his book with a charming final chapter of aphoristic desserts, entitled "Commonplaces." His own performance now done, the musician greets his clamoring audience backstage with a grin and sends them off with *petit* literary *bon-bons* to savor post-concert. After-dinner mints on the way out the door, some for succour now, others for consideration later.

***

To the delight of this pianist, *Notes on the Piano* is one of those rare books on my shelf that never seems to grow old, regardless of countless readings. It will always remain in my personal top ten list of indispensable books for the pianist. Certainly there are unforgettable autobiographies by important pianists whose stories captivate wholly—those of Louis Moreau Gottschalk, Artur Rubinstein and Claudio Arrau come to mind—and copious volumes of ingenious pianistic advice from sages like Ferruccio Busoni, Josef Hofmann, Russell Sherman, and many more. But literary works that elevate the art of piano playing into the sphere of true philosophic discovery are indeed rare. Ernst Bacon succeeded as a writer as he likewise succeeded as a composer. In being ruggedly true to his own vision, inspired as he was by so many art forms outside and around music, and by the nature of which he felt himself an integral part. In preserving that unique and invigorating outlook within the pages of this book, he gave us a volume to be treasured by every person who reads it—those who begin their every morning to a metronome at the quarter-84, stretching digits over keys black and white, as well as the many more who do not.

SARA DAVIS BUECHNER
*Vancouver, B.C., Canada*
*April 2011*

Ms. Buechner thanks the following sources for information used in assembling this Introduction:

The Ernst Bacon Society: www.ernstbacon.org
The Online Archive of California: www.oac.cdlib.org
The Syracuse University Library: www.library.syr.edu
The Howard Gotlieb Archival Research Center at Boston University: www.bu.edu
Song of America: www.songofamerica.net

# CONTENTS

# Introductory

*The last thing we find in making a book*
*is to know what we must put in first.*

B. PASCAL

This is a book to be nibbled. Open it wherever you like, for its thought is not successive nor cumulative. Its last chapter could as well be its first. It consists of notes gathered by the way of music-making. These range from narrow to broad, specific to general, technical to musical, recondite to obvious. They are variants on some underlying theme which does not appear, and which has not disclosed itself fully to me. They assume the prerogative of variations; to repeat, restate, stress, embellish and even contradict their theme. Yet they leave out more than they take in.

They are for those who understand them, and are meant to clarify rather than inform. If they contain information, it is mostly for those already informed. They teach what is known, but not as a text. Music was seldom learned from a book, and the best of musicians rarely troubled to organize in book form what they knew. They taught by example and often they learned much from nonmusical sources. Music, to have life, must be practiced; to have health, must not become ingrown. Music is not music's only soil.

The piano is my point of departure. I go out from it into music, and then again return to the piano, laying on it the parental burdens of the art. The piano has stout legs, and will outlast many disparagements.

My credentials are in part a lingering amateurism; that is to say, a love that resists too much learning. I have always avoided acquiring more erudition than was necessary. A little learning is a good thing, but too large a learning begets a taste for more and more, and before you know it, the ambition to know overcomes the desire to do, first embarrassing it, then bullying it into hiding.

We know too much already about music, and care too little about our musicians, the living ones. So much concern for the distant and the past can only be purchased by a neglect of the present and the near. It is true we have schools, more than enough. But our learning treats of the past as a fact, and of the present as a fiction.

Educated music has been made to be a counter-eddy to the fast stream of present life. Its tenets are precisely the opposite to the tenets by which we otherwise live. It is apologetic, unproud, timorous, hysterical, recondite, un-nativist, perverse, effeminate, vitiated, and spoiled. It lacks integrity, courage, exercise, masculinity (femininity, too), vigor, poetry, religiousness, and optimism.

The piano has for centuries invaded nearly all music. Most of the masters were pianists. Nearly all music then, must concern the piano no less. It is idle to speak of the art's organization, its sociology, its pedagogy, its economics; of its composers, singers, fiddlers, its orchestras and chamber groups, without involving somehow the piano. Accordingly I have more than touched on many musical matters that tell nothing of how the piano is manipulated, but which tell a great deal about why it is played as it is, and even why it is not played as, and where, it should be. There is no end to its ramifications. It is still music's headquarters.

The book has some polemics. But most opposition, I find, hangs more on how a thing is said than on what is said. If I have occasionally indulged in some diplomatic slight or insult, and seem to take pleasure in others' pain, it is only to remind them of the pain they have long given us, in stripping music of its natural pleasures. For they have robbed and deflowered it of innocence, have unclothed it of mysteries, and indiscriminately advertised its intimate secrets. There is no aspect of music, not even the artists' private gods and angels (all those cherished, hidden puerilities to which the best have turned for whispered oracles) that is not subject to an obstetrical and psychological appraisal, or to class-gossip within the academic army of the unemployed, or worst of all, to a shameless packaged ubiquity, not for purposes of pleasure or education, but to fill out time that needs filling, and to fill the vacuum of expectation and curiosity contrived to fill vast and many pockets.

Now everyone asks what is the secret of creation. In the very telling it would already be lost, could it be told. The question has the same impertinence as asking, "What is your private life?" One must earn the right to put such questions. "There is more power and beauty in the well-kept secret of one's self and one's thoughts," said Matthew Arnold, "than in the display of a whole heaven that one may have inside one." We are not all of us Freudians, and it is no disrespect to science to hold that we are more interested in the art than in its explanation, when that threatens to explain it away.

Music is full of secrets. They may be shared by many, yet sparingly told. If you intend to do a great or beautiful thing, it is best you remain silent about it until it is done, for who but yourself could know what is involved? It is a good superstition to keep your plans under wraps, the more so the better they are. I intend to divulge no secrets, but will speak much of working habits, listening habits, playing habits; and hint at profitable devices for self-encouragement, even for advantageous self-deception, in the business of learning.

My "Commonplaces" have given me some pleasure in their compression and succinctness, although in formulating them I was, in the words of Franklin's Poor Richard, "conscious that not a tenth part of the wisdom was my own, . . . but rather the gleanings I had made of the sense of ages and nations."

One notes what one is ready for. Art has no patents nor has philosophy; only its lawyers and bureaucrats are forever discovering infringements. If art recognized patents, all the great would be transgressors. The most original thing a man can do is to rediscover the hidden mainstream of his language, recapture for his day immemorial familiarities in it, and search out the most appropriate dialect in which to say his say.

In short, the book is about the piano in music, or about music in the piano, I can't say which the more.

I have said as much about what is wrong with our music as about what is right. I did so because most of the talk in print goes the other way. But I know of no wrong that could not easily have been righted, if faced in time, and that cannot be righted, even today, given an outlay of moral courage as great as the present income in profits. Who is prepared to risk boycott from the powers rather than bow to "expediency"?

"You alone will not reform things" is one of those insidious truths that forgets to add, "But others will join, once you take a stand."

Even so, music is really not very important beside politics, astro-mechanics, the cold war of social dogma. *It will have no voice in the world's morals, so long as it has no morality itself.* Like Archimedes' lever, music, could move the world if it would. But then it will have to be more than just a pretty or problematic thing, ready to yield to every zephyr of coterie or style.

"How does the poet speak to men with power," said Carlyle, "but by being still more a man than they."

# THE
# PERFORMER

\*

# *Of*
## *Interpretation*

*An artist should never lose sight of the thing as a whole. He who puts too much into details will find that the thread which holds the whole thing together will break.* F. CHOPIN

Like the actor and the stage director, the interpreter stands as middleman between the writer and his public. All depends on him. The more unique is the work, the more convincing must be its reading. There are canons of originality no less than of conformance, to unsettle which requires the most skillful advocacy. When Chopin sounds badly, the pianist is at fault. But when John Smith's music sounds badly, Smith alone is blamed.

*The performing art may represent today a level superior to that of the writing art.* As against the anarchic confusion existing in the composing field, the standards in performance are technically higher and more fixed than ever before. Whoever chooses novelty in writing is allowed to be innocent until proven guilty. But in performance, a deviator is adjudged guilty until he proves his innocence. Never before was performance as disciplined as today: never was writing less so.

It was no accident that Chopin included two of his finest nocturnes in his book of etudes. It is interesting that the piano, an instrument of percussion, should have gained so large a share of the literature of *melodic* music. Quite probably this is because it is capable like no other instrument of combining harmony with melody, is complete in itself, and does not suffer the organ's limitation of tone. The artful grading of the piano's *percussive* tones, as to length, loudness, timing, delay and haste, and all the relations of melody to accompaniment or countermelody; these together with pedalling, make possible the piano's illusion of continuous and expressive melody.

The piano's resonance does not stop with the piano itself, as anyone knows who has played out of doors. The entire hall is involved in its vibrations. Since the player cannot remove himself from the origin of his sound, he can hope to hear himself as others hear him only through electrical devices, or by exercise of his imagination. There is every reason to think that the greatest artists have given thought and ear to producing sounds that fill and carry the best in whatever hall is at hand. I have heard Kreisler, alone with his little Guarnerius, fill a colosseum in which a large orchestra tried vainly to conquer its vacuous immensity. One must know the point beyond which the enlargement of tone is not only useless but harmful. The ear of the listener adjusts easily to all levels, and is ready to accept lesser sounds as climactic, so long as they are proportioned to other sounds. Segovia's unamplified guitar will prove this. *It is quality that carries where quantity fails;* the imagination defeating decibels.

Any extreme; of slow or fast, rough or smooth, soft or loud, goes with a heightened tension. *Middle ground is middle effort.* The lazy player can no more achieve a pianissimo than a fortissimo, a largo than a presto. There is nothing more demanding than a sustained slow tempo unless it be an expressive dolcissimo. Alexander Raab remarked that Toscanini showed his age, in his vigorous middle eighties, only in that the tempos of his slow movements were not quite so slow as before. If there is one trait common to all great interpreters, it is their *capacity for intensification.* There are many ways to achieve intensity, dictated by the music; but whether explosive, impassioned, eloquent or restrained, intensity will always be felt as a mark of inner energy. Without this intensity, the listener never more than half listens. But when it is there, his attention is drawn in ratio to the player's concentration; he feels what the player communicates, on whatever level it may be.

We are content if the singer is master of but one category of singing. Thus we designate the voice as lyric, dramatic, coloratura and the like. But the pianist is expected to be all of these, and his preparation embraces all styles. In point of fact, his best gifts are as circumscribed as those of the singer; and by confining himself to his own special sphere of playing he may surpass those who essay to do all. A full mastery of but one idiom may represent more breadth than a versatile, and necessarily shallower, proficiency in all idioms. *There is breadth in depth,* no less than depth in breadth. Some travel most profitably at home.

Nevertheless, the discovery of what is one's own special sphere of music should not be hastened; rather it should grow out of a wide range of trial and effort, particularly among those of student age. It is best to settle down after one has seen something of the world.

Great virtuosity should not be made an absolute condition of a pianist's acceptance as artist, any more than mere power, range, or skill in fioritura, on the part of the singer. He may have exceptional tonal, melodic, coloristic, or imaginative qualities which deserve acclaim, the more so in an age in which facility has become common currency.

*The whole rule of rubato is grace.* Every increase and decrease of tempo has to do with the demands of declamation: phrasing, words (if any), accents, rests, harmony, and all the idiosyncrasies of instruments (such as the crossing of strings in the violin, breathing in the winds, securing the pedal base in the piano, allowing for extended leaps, and other undue manual difficulties). The rubato has also to do with the dimension of a work, a large work normally concluding with a longer allargando, for example, than a small one, just as a freight train takes longer to come to a stop than a motor car. An abruptness is allowable only when it is meaningful. A jerky or irregular increase or decrease in tempo is a misdemeanor, and reveals an insecurity of control, as with an adult who cannot walk steadily. Some music is all rubato, as is much of Puccini. Other music comes as close as is humanly possible to metronomic regularity, as does nearly all dance music, which expresses the body's pleasure in a regular, measured movement.

The declamation of music seldom permits the hastening of a beat, but is continually calling for delay. A *delay* calls attention to itself and is, in some degree, emphatic. On the piano this delay is mostly effected with both hands together, but sometimes it takes the form of the melody note following its chord, or accompaniment. This latter has the effect of *warming* the tone, as with an imaginary vibrato, or else it suggests the singer's portamento. But a continuous delaying of melody notes can easily become a sentimentality or mannerism.

Embellishments stemming from a time before they were written out are a large subject, best studied in C. P. E. Bach, Quantz and Leopold Mozart. The pianist of today is not obliged to abide *literally* by the instructions of these masters, conceived as they were for other times, tastes and instruments; but he should learn them before permitting himself liberties. The modern piano, differing from its predecessors in power, sustainment of tone and pedal, poses new approaches. In general, it invites less decoration, and tends toward simplification, just as the more powerful orchestra and the organ of earlier times were treated more simply than the fragile and voluble clavichord or harpsichord.

To preserve the spirit of embellishment may require a deviation from the letter.

The quality of a turn tells me a great deal about an interpreter. A first-class carpenter should also be a first-class cabinet-maker, and shows his craft in the delicacy no less than the doughtiness of his structures. Elizabeth Schumann could make the littlest turn in, say, Schubert's "Litanei" a moment of sheerest poetry. Some pianists of otherwise large abilities can make a turn seem like a footnote.

Dullness, remarked Liszt, is the cardinal sin of performance. Nothing contributes to this more than the ostentation of learning, whereby a player will emphasize and sometimes exaggerate structural details, phrasings and dynamics, in a spirit of zealous didacticism or reform. He imagines that the listener is more interested in a work's wiring and plumbing than in its purpose and poetry. The homiletic virtuoso has been made very fashionable of late. It becomes more important that the public distinguish between the Baroque and the Biedermeier than that it should be awed by what Schopenhauer described as Beethoven's power to "thunder on the flute," or be allowed to overhear, in Lao-tzu's words, "stone growing on a cliff."

As in all else, accents are purely relative, and proportioned to that which surrounds them. Almost anything very sudden is an accent, even a sudden drop in tone. There are accents by *expectation* (mostly as a result of sequential patterns), and there are accents by *surprise*. An accent is like a cliff in the landscape.

Not many know how to play a true piano bass. It is not enough to pedal it clean; it must be savored. Paderewski gave us to hear the noble snarl of a Steinway bass. Koussevitzky had a special ear for deep sounds in the orchestra. Rachmaninoff understood basses. The piano bass has a masculine ring, and is the nearest thing we have to the ancient gongs of China. Its dignity will not be hastened. Given the pedal, it picks up a family of overtones and, grandfather-like, it resolves all the high-pitched contending sounds into harmoniousness, through its common ancestral bond.

The experienced pianist will mostly underplay, however slightly, his biggest moments. Giving all, has the effect of over-playing, and gives away the secret of power, whose limit is never fully known to the listener, when it is not fully revealed. Monadnock, wrapped in a cap of clouds, could be the Grand Teton.

While an older author occasionally would write beyond his instruments, in range, power, sustainment, or character, anticipating developments beyond his time, the nature of music was, of course, largely determined by the instruments of the day. This knowledge should affect our present interpretation of older works. A Mozart or a Scarlatti forte is not a Brahms forte, and deserves to be played crisply rather than weightily. Similarly, in pedalling, the earlier music should eschew too large sonorities, particularly on accented chords, when followed by their own arpeggiations, in which the rapid separate pulsations deserve more definition than the chords and basses from which they are generated. The lack of sustainment of the early instruments automatically took care of this.

Beethoven introduced orchestral quality, as well as new power, into the piano. In performing his music, the player, unlike the conductor who drives his orchestra to achieve its utmost in sound and fury, must learn to temper his exertions within the limits of physical elasticity. It requires but a few moments of playing to the full, to tire the hand or the wrist beyond the point where its sensitivity may be recovered. When music invites the extremes of power, the player must let élan take the place of brute force.

Much music after Beethoven poses similar problems of a power-level which, if literally sustained, would exhaust the player. It is as with the distance runner who may, through tempering his speed by only the littlest fraction, sustain his pace over a long period—while if he drives himself to the limit for only a moment, he cannot hope to survive the race.

The tendency to hasten a crescendo and retard a diminuendo is universal. If all other disciplines fail in overcoming this fault, one may consciously practice to exaggeration the contrary; that is, deliberately retard the rising, and accelerate the falling sound. The discipline of ensemble is another corrective.

The player should consider that in all speech, an *increasing emphasis calls for added deliberation,* and that a relaxation of mood brings an easing of pace, which is, after such deliberation, a tempo increase.

"A really good playwright," says Frank O'Connor, "will give you a part that you can do with what you like." Now, as a reaction to the license of the past, we hog-tie the interpreter with the fetish of "fidelity to the score," and as a result, we have an art as static as was the former extravagant. This new idolomania of the composer is the more fatuous since he is in effect today on the bottom rung of the importances. Music is not served by enslaving one of its parties to another. Of course the performer serves the author; but whom does the author serve, if not the performer?

Tension, so easily achieved by the voice or the strings, is created on the piano mainly through certain discreet exaggerations, as between melody and accompaniment, or between louder and softer, or with rubati, or with the holding or delaying of tones, as often called for in pedalling. Tension is often achieved by a high degree of precision.

Not to invest music with a sentiment which is not there is as important as to give music the sentiment it already has. Sounds have their bleak and barren moments, their treeless, shrubless, waterless areas, that call for the chilly, or the dry, or the expressionless. In these is often a gray comfort, deeper than can be supplied by the warmest opulence. An arctic solitude offers sometimes the best solace. Must we blow over such a scene the sensuous vibrato of the strings, or try to relieve its coldness with a rich, warm piano tone, or invade its frozenness with shimmering flute sounds, by which the player thinks to bring the feathered creatures of the air? Why not let cold music sing its coldness?

The rubato is not only inseparably tied together with music's declamation, but is a part of all instrumental athleticism. Extreme rapidity calls sometimes for a running start, which is to say, *a rubato of acceleration*. This is where the orchestra differs from the solo instrument; for the art of orchestration will always provide the most dexterous instruments for rapid passages, and not burden these with obstacles before they enter on their assignment of brilliance. A taxing orchestral work, well scored, is full of brief recesses for every group. The pianist, being an entire orchestra himself, enjoys no such respites, and must compensate for their lack with occasional freedoms of tempo. Like the hurdler or obstacle racer, he cannot maintain the sprinter's unvaried pace.

I observe the nature of a crescendo: whether it is continuous or interrupted; whether it is controlled or casual; whether it climbs at a steady pitch, or follows a steepening curve, or else a lessening one; whether its climax is gentle or precipitate. All these curves have their counterparts in the profiles of hills and mountains. The diminuendo has these same variants in reverse, and it by no means follows that the fall must have the same curve as the rise. It is only the volcano that is symmetrical in cross section.

Toscanini had the faculty of controlling rising and falling lines of sound. Therein lay much of his power. His was a gift of simplification, of almost abstracting music to its topographic and climatic essentials. His powers showed the greatest on the highest ranges of music. Thus he was supreme in Beethoven, in Verdi, in Brahms and in Wagner, all masters of grand tonal topography. It takes a man to stand up to such men.

The nature of a staccato remains an ever unsettled question. Doubtless, had Thomas Edison had his way, musical notation in this, as in other respects, would have achieved more exactitude. But Edison was a man of genius with machines, and not the arts, and could not possibly understand the advantage an art enjoys in being put not too literally on record. Music will have to meet the changing needs of instruments, tastes, capacities and uses, in the future. The guesswork of each generation as regards the intentions of previous generations makes the study of older works more interesting than were they corralled in sterner rules of action. One of the good things in Shakespeare is that he left us no rules whatever.

All we can say about dotted notes is that they are meant to be detached, but as to how much, there is no clue. String players and conductors are little agreed as between the short staccato on the string and that with the bouncing bow. Staccatos on the piano may be plucked off the key, in the manner of a pizzicato; they may be rapped, either from the wrist or the finger, or they may be played in any degree of *detaché*, with a rebounding wrist, pointedly or yieldingly, or anything in between. Some music uses dots over notes which are also connected by slurs or with the pedal, indicating a connected sound with unconnected motions.

Between all these possibilities, the player must decide, whether guided by editings, traditions, the example of others, or his own preferences. Let him take consolation in his uncertainty, in the thought that any choice is better than none, and will justify itself by virtue of consistency.

Sporadic pedallings during staccatos need discretion, inasmuch as they produce a resonance sharply in contrast with the unpedalled staccatos.

How you begin a piece is everything. It is in the first bar that you establish your art with the listener. Some there are who arrive at their tempo and tone level only after some desultory bars have passed. Such vacillation proves to be costly. There remains more to recover than has been lost; like reestablishing a good name after a misdeed.

Many there are who do not know how to end a piece. The commonest vice is to throw away a conclusion, in a spirit of abandonment, as if the player had decided the final chords are superfluous, and will hold no interest for the listener. And indeed they will not when thrown away in that fashion. Comparing, let us say, the long reiteration of tonic chords at the end of Beethoven's *C Minor Symphony* with the sparse endings in his later works, the very suspicion of redundance in the former makes it the more necessary to give it conviction. Would you accuse Beethoven of overstatement? Your accusation could only fall heavily back on you.

I know of no such thing as a correct tempo. To begin with, the old indications, andante, largo, allegro, are descriptive more of character than of tempo. What, for example, could be the meaning of andantino? A lesser andante; but since andante is the nearest term we have to a neutral tempo, does andantino mean less fast or less slow, or indeed, less neither? And yet somehow we grasp its meaning in context. When, in Beethoven's day, the metronome was introduced, it proved not very reliable by modern measurements. Since then, the instruments, the auditoriums, the technical levels, and the concepts of music, even its pitch, have all changed, affecting tempo as well as every other factor of interpretation. Finally, there is the player or conductor who is, fortunately, also not a standard object; who cannot be himself by being only a product of rules, a composite of tastes.

A proper tempo is one that is appropriate to every element of a performance—the work itself, the player with all the facets of his personality, including also his technical capacity, the place, the acoustics, the occasion, perhaps even the time of day, and certainly the audience.

Complicated as all this seems, it is in fact a simple matter if the interpreter allows himself to rely more on intuition than on statute and willful calculation.

Translating music from another age into our own is a subtle matter. The score, unlike the painting, is but a plan—an approximation. Now we have the phonograph record, enabling Stravinsky, Rachmaninoff, Prokofiev, and Bloch to give to the future their own "definitive" versions. But what will time do to these? And what would time not do to their authors, were it possible to transplant them into a future day?

"Were a genius like Mozart to be born today," said Schumann, "he would perhaps write concertos in the manner of Chopin rather than the manner of Mozart." He would give himself new latitudes of dimension, rubato, and color. He would then be living in the immense shadow of Beethoven, and be aware of the new audacities of Berlioz and Liszt, conscious of the growing democracy of America, and touched by the new beauties Schubert evolved out of an older

Mozart. It is a speculation as endless as it is useless, but it awakens some doubt as to the propriety of being too exacting with coming generations, of presuming too much on their taste, of jumping off the stage of the present into the audience of the future.

The predominance of the orchestra in recent music has affected the character of all solo performance. In the days of Caruso, Paderewski, Ysaye, Busoni and Chaliapin, when soloists were the reigning stars, orchestras were inclined to be more indulgent toward soloistic idiosyncrasies. Today the conductor is supreme, and orchestral interpretation takes the lead. Orchestras having little call to make rubati on technical grounds, a more austere and inflexible tempo prevails, and this invades solo performance as well, sometimes to the detriment of its technical and even its expressive needs. Adherents of this view pride themselves on their "fidelity." They forget that solo music was written by instrumentalists, who must themselves have conceived it in the framework of its own technical requirements, which are not those of an orchestra.

No one did more in our day than Toscanini to reestablish the integrity of the score, to strip interpretation of the accumulated barnacles of sentimentality and caprice, and to fasten a high responsibility on the interpreter. But the reforms of a great reformer are not always those of his imitators. The probity of Toscanini has turned into a prudery of score-worship, whereby conductors often bully their betters into easy and unfair submission. After all, the score is only the score. "The written note," observes Casals, "is like a strait jacket, whereas music is, like life itself, in constant movement."

"Brilliance," while it may be compounded of either, is neither speed nor loudness alone. Speed beyond a certain point defeats itself. Successive sounds, when very fast, begin to be grouped in the mind, and lose their character of individual pulsation. A well-articulated, fairly rapid passage may give more impression of swiftness than a faster passage played beyond all perception of its swift detail. Likewise, a large sound, pushed beyond its limits of sonority, will become harsh and defeat itself in acoustical corrugation. Brilliance in the piano entails control, pedalling, appropriate accenting, even enunciation and a suitable proportioning of dynamics. There are good pianists who cannot play brilliantly, and brilliant pianists who do not make good music. By and large, however, the term brilliance is overused, and indeed music has better things to offer than mere brilliance.

No great art is without ecstasy. Many look upon this ecstasy as some kind of vacation-land, some Shangri-la or Tahiti, open to all upon proper payment, but the benefits of which they will forego until the more serious business of life has been attended to (fortune, security, the gold-strike). They intend some day to enjoy its blisses, heedless of its tribulations. They do not know that the cultivation of fervent moods is virtually a professional duty of the artist. Ecstasy is his business. He is not a holiday fisherman and will jealously guard the waters of his spirit against drought or pollution. This is one reason for his despair over the inescapable ubiquity of music today (good and bad both: the better the music, the worse its irresponsible overuse. Waste is the forerunner of atrophy.)

What is it today that makes silence the costliest of luxuries? It is as if plain water could be afforded only by the rich, while all the rest must still their thirst forsooth with beer and Coca Cola.

As with the swimmer and the runner, endurance, too, must be practiced. However much you may harbor your resources and control your speed and power, you will on occasion encounter the pain of fatigue. In practice you relieve it with an interruption; but in performance you must endure it with no visible sign of distress. The listener is there to enjoy the music, not to witness your agonies of perseverance.

In the appoggiatura, decoration for once goes right into the heart of expression, and becomes essential to it. Defined as a note foreign to the chord, adjacent to it, above or below, the real meaning of the word is that of *a note leaned upon*. It is, indeed, a built-in dissonance on a strong beat resolving into consonance, or relative consonance, on a weak beat, and symbolizes more simply than any other device the passage from strain to release, from ingress to egress, from pressure to yield, pain to rest, effort to repose, violence to moderation, and energy to languor. It has great meaning. Beethoven turned to its use increasingly as he grew older, and sought ways to speak his more compassionate lines. The nineteenth century is never without it. Wagner and Chopin, emptied of appoggiatura, would be nothing.

To know a work fully is to have formed a large habit compounded of many lesser ones. What goes before and what comes after affect what is in between. This sense of before-ness and after-ness belongs not only to a detail, but to a phrase, a section, a movement, an entire work, and indeed to a whole program. The composer, having this sense, extends it into his entire life and career. It becomes a part of the historical sense.

Music is all proportion. A succession of but two chords involves proportion. A rhythm is a proportion. Two tones of a melody already make a proportion. The sounds within a simple chord are proportioned. Every form, every dimension, every register, color, cadence, tempo, dynamic—each of these contains or makes proportions. One may isolate any one of these elements and arrive at a hint of its psychology. But the entire work: who will presume to explain it all? As well give a final definition of beauty.

We recognize what we cannot explain. We can say what it is not, but not what it is. *We sense better than we reason.*

It is sometimes said that a man should be able to "play a work in his sleep," meaning that his playing should have become so automatic that it will go on of itself easier than stop. There is little virtue in this, if the automation is only of the hands. But if it includes the invocation of intensity and feeling also, if the routine involves thought, that is something else.

Nevertheless, the best performance will mostly exceed the limits of safety. Only a dull performance is safe. The superior artist, if he has made safe a certain achievement, however high, will immediately attempt new hazards of eloquence.

*The purpose of practice is not to reduce consciousness but to heighten it.* One climbs a mountain for the exhilaration of achievement, and not to find sleep at its summit.

A steady tempo is at the root of all rubati. It is the prairie from which the mountains stand forth. "In the equanimity of music lies its divinity," said Thoreau, giving voice to the trunk of a truth, which has however many branches.

Most people have a tendency to slow down or to speed up, and few are given to controlling a steady tempo (not therefore a metronomic one), which becomes then the most basic of disciplines.

"I am always learning," said Casals; meaning that the discoveries in music, as in nature, never come to an end. Give a work a rest and it will sprout new leaves and fruits when you return to it. Each new discovery adds to your store of wisdom. And so, in the end, the work of a master becomes your own, and indeed you. And you come as close to Beethoven as did he himself, and with a great deal more patience and charity.

Most interpreters, singers as well as instrumentalists, find it easier to make melody come alive loudly than softly. The main thing toward creating soft melody, is to *want it*. But wanting sometimes follows inadvertently on doing, provided there is the discernment to recognize the arrival. Whether wanting or doing comes first is never settled, but it need also not be. Nevertheless, it is a great moment in an artist's growth when he discovers the magic of delicate sounds, and then again when he learns the carrying power of such whisperings in even the largest halls, the audience cooperating with instant silence the moment they arrive.

An artist needs acknowledgment not only to please his vanity, but also to measure his art against his public and his day. A little failure is a good thing, but a failure such as many of our best talents (I should say most of them) suffer, marks the failure of our society.

# *ii*

# *Of*
# *Melody*

*Drawing is the probity of Art.*     M. INGRES

By itself the single piano tone is nothing. It acquires meaning only when it is related to other tones. The tone is a product of three factors, the manner of *depressing the keys,* the *proportioning* to other tones, both vertically and horizontally, and the *pedalling.* It is often said that once the tone has been sounded all movement thereafter is wasted. But the gesture of tone production includes release as well as attack. The pianist "follows through" in making a sound, no less than the baseball pitcher follows through his throw, even after the ball has left his hand. It is the entire gesture, however small, that makes the tone.

*Vertically* speaking, the voices of a chord are seldom equal. Normally the melody tone is predominant. Next in strength is the bass. The remaining sounds are less pronounced. Melody being mostly at the top, this corresponds roughly to the proportioning of the string sections in the orchestra and of the choirs in a chorus, wherein the top and bottom are usually the strongest. The proper tone normally lies somewhere between melodic preponderance and harmonic sonority.

*Horizontally* speaking, the relation of successive sounds is what produces melodic flow, gives the impression of tonal continuity, and compensates for the absence of the tonal modulation and enrichment characteristic of the singing instruments and the voice. A series of percussions, such as the piano produces, since it cannot make for continuous sound, can only simulate it. Thus the effectiveness of a piano melody lies in its power of suggestion. A piano melody is like a graph that is smoothly drawn to connect a series of points. The fidelity with which this graph is drawn is what gives it grace and meaning. Lacking any means to alter or enrich the separate tone, piano melody invites more differentiation between the tones than is common with instruments making sustained sounds.

The melodist sings through his fingers. He draws his line into, and away from, the peaks of intensity; and indeed most melodies have such summits, however steep or gentle. He conveys the singer's very breathing, if not actually separating his phrases (the very thought is often enough). He is mindful of the slight delay the voice requires in making a large leap from low to high or high to low. He conveys the slur and the portamento, sometimes with a *delay*, sometimes with an overlapping of pedal sounds, sometimes with a drop in sound; quite often with some or all of these together.

Sometimes he presses the keys, clinging to them as firmly as a violinist to his strings. At other times he lets his fingers drop liquidly into the notes, *allowing* more than *urging* them. At all times his hand is deft and its pressure elastic.

His tones vary more than a singer's. The small exaggerations make up for his lack of power to sustain, swell, or enrich a tone through the vibrato. His longer tones receive just enough added pressure to equalize them with his shorter tones, but never so much as to make the device obvious.

If a level is to be maintained, in which the tones are of unequal duration, they will be played unequally to the point where they create a level effect. A group of rapid tones, such as an embellishment, mordent or trill, will be played below the melody's level, so as not to sound above it. For, however smoothly the pianist may play, he is still using percussions which, by very nature, raise the level of sound the closer they are grouped together. With the violin, a dozen notes produced on one bow of given duration will yield no more sound than a single note produced on a bow of the same duration, given the same pressure. But a dozen notes played on the piano will very much outsound one single note sustained for the same time and played with the same pressure. It is to equalize this inequality that the melodist strives, even if unconsciously. The equalization is one of effect, and is by no means literal.

The melodist is particularly careful of the first note of a phrase, especially in the event of an up-beat. His descending hand must produce no inadvertent initial accent. Indeed he mostly learns to lay his hand on the keys silently before beginning (unlike most organists, who fear an accidental sound, because of the light pressure of organ manuals). He does this not only to avoid an initial impact but as a habit of orientation, leaving his eye free to follow what may be an accompaniment demanding watching. Like the singer who harbors his breath, he cultivates an economy of movement in keeping with the smooth sounds he intends to make, and which will sound the smoother when *seen* also as smooth.

As in speech, in which a syllable of importance is sometimes delayed or held, he will delay or hold significant notes, but never so much as to destroy his essential rhythm, or distort a rubato. At times he will permit his accompaniment to go *with* these delays; at other times he will allow it to proceed regularly *in contrast to* his melodic rubato.

Permitting the melody note to follow after the bass, or even breaking the chord has the effect of *warming* the tone. To do this continually would result in an affectation, worse than the austerity of doing it not at all. Like the portamento of the singer or the slide of the string player, too much makes for sentimentality, while too little makes for coldness. Hastenings will be treated the same as delays, but they are rarer.

In sustained melody, the melodist will incline *to stretch the shortest notes imperceptibly,* so as to increase their drag and therewith the over-all tension, to more nearly equalize them with the longer notes, and overcome the piano's tendency toward glibness. In music of an emphatic or rhythmic sort (such as marches, gigues, polonaises, boleros, waltzes, etc.), he will sharpen the rhythm, (sometimes simulating the drum-like nature of the metric pattern) by imperceptibly compressing the short notes making suitable compensation for this in the long and more accented notes. Some syncopation calls for a slight delay to overcome a certain ragging effect. In all these minute alterations, his aim will be to create the *impression* of what is meant by a suitable digression from literal *fact.*

If his chief melody is not at the top, but in the bass. or in the middle register, it may need slightly more than the usual preponderance, since the listener is used to expecting the melody at the top. If the melody is doubled (in octaves, thirds, sixths, etc.), the lower line of the doubling should ordinarily be subordinated to the upper, to avoid thickening and to add lustre. Nevertheless, especially in doublings at two-octave intervals, of the kind used by Schumann, and also by Mozart in certain four-hand works, there may be reason to allow the lower line to predominate, for the sake of richness. It is seldom that parallelisms deserve to be played equally.

As between melody and accompaniment, it is better to exaggerate their difference than to minimize it. However, the restraint of the introvert, often described as a failure of power of "projection," sometimes bespeaks a sensitivity that is preferable to the overemphasis of the extrovert.

The pianist's best school of melody is the singer. Apart from hearing singers and their recordings, he should work with them as accompanist and coach. Good singers are good self-listeners, and what they often lack in knowledge and "musicianship" (by which is meant the academic virtues of accuracy, factual affluence and ready solfeggio), they make up for in a surer intuition, and a flair for dramatic characterization. They make sounds often in a state of self-intoxication. While they rely on the pianist for guidance and support, the pianist can learn from them about melody in its freest and most native form. The good accompanist or coach tends to sing along inwardly with the singer, the while he adds his accompaniment. *The voice is the source, the piano gives direction.* Together they make a profitable union.

A note receives importance, or is made to be important, through its length, its altitude (sometimes the reverse), its strength, its position in the bar, its color (whether by harmony or instrumentation), its irregularity (such as its being a syncopation, accent, or the result of a leap), and its position at the crown of a phrase. The musical author, without conscious thought, normally causes important syllables of poetry to coincide with any, all, or some of these devices, when writing vocal music. In instrumental melody, the vocal parentage is felt, but the range becomes greater, and the limitations are fewer.

The national characteristics of language show themselves in instrumental as well as in vocal melody. In French, the accentuation is more by length than stress, by comparison with English. English inclines more to syncopation than German. Swedish has a greater fluctuation up-and-down than English. German has a weightier quality than any

Mediterranean tongue. Hungarian is characterized by initial accents. In Russian we are unduly aware of rugged consonants. As compared with Italian, English is diphthongmatic. The English of our South sings its vowels far more than does Yankee English. The musician, once he is made conscious of these, and other language characteristics, will discover them as factors in national "style," even apart from vocal music; and this will add to the wisdom of his declamation.

Some singers, possessed of beautiful voices, fail not only to convey their words, but to realize the beauty of their color, as it affects their singing tones. Failing then with the music of poetry, they lose not a little of the poetry of the music. No worthy composer would use verse merely to hang a song onto. It is possible that his melody may go in search of words, instead of the usual contrary. But words, to him, are meaningful, in sound no less than intent.

Good diction, then, is clarity and musicality both, and yet it must not be so marked as to injure melody through overemphasis. Nothing is worse than the singer who mouths and articulates his consonances so scrupulously as to ruin the flow of his melody. Certainly, de-worded song is to be preferred to de-melodized words, if indeed he must choose.

And again with pianists, many have given no more thought to song than have the singers to poetry. Not that they need imagine words to their piano melodies, but they should learn to conceive, shape and even *breathe their melodies vocally*.

The common avocal approach of pianists is particularly apparent in the playing of fioriture and recitative-like passages, so dear to Beethoven in his later writing, so frequent in Liszt, Chopin and even Brahms (suggestive sometimes of opera), and so eloquent in some of Bach's fantasias.

Melody involves a study of its accompaniment. Only over the most perfect of backgrounds may the line of melody rest with grace. The simplest little Alberti bass merits thought as regards its regularity, its quality (whether legato, leggiero or staccato), its pedalling (or non-pedal), the relative strength of its bass notes, its whole relation to melody, whether one of *support* or of *contrast*.

Once an accompaniment has received proper attention, it will recede to a role of subordination, as a willing and educated servant.

*The more thought has gone into the accompaniment, the freer then is the thought for the melody.*

Considered in a painter's terms, Robert Henri remarked: "A background is not to be neglected. It is a structural factor. . . . The background must travel along and keep pace with every advance of the picture. . . . A weak background is a deadly thing. . . . Many an artist has fussed all day over a face . . . never getting it right because the fault should have been found in the background."

A melody is like the outline of a range of hills. The table landscape of the Western desert, in which one level mesa after another is seen receding into the distance, suggests varying levels of sound, with little transition from one to another. This topography of levels is more characteristic of the harpsichord and the organ than of the piano, but is by no means outside the piano's range, as well.

Most melody, however, is an ever-varying, never repeating curve. The loftiest mountains, if one could see them in cross section, are mostly steeper in the higher reaches. Beethoven's extreme and often precipitate dynamics give his music a sombre and high-Alpine quality. His is a music so dramatic it needs no added drama. Mozart represents a gentler and more cultivated landscape; while in Handel and Bach, the mountains tower, but less frowningly. The great mountains of music mostly have eternal snow.

A polyphonic style can be cultivated by a discipline of bringing out each of the voices involved, the while subduing all the others. This should be done in a legato, and is better achieved by reducing the lesser voices than by exaggerating the one made salient (just as the painter brings out areas of light by deepening the tones of his surrounding shadows, rather than by adding white). Legato is always enhanced by softness, for *the louder the piano tone, the more does it become percussive.*

Through this discipline the ear gets to hear and know each part along with its counterpart, and the hand acquires the art of controlling different levels simultaneously, a faculty useful in nonpolyphonic music as well. Until this is smoothly achieved with each part, irrespective of its relative importance, the discipline is not complete. Once it is, the player has then the means to shift emphasis from one voice to another as the music requires, with the same ease as a conductor regulating the choirs of his chorus or orchestra.

While polyphony means to most people an equality of voices, it should not be construed as a constant equality; on the contrary, polyphony invites a shifting predominance of voices, each having its say at the appropriate time. As in conversation the listener frames the speaker, so in counterpoint does the subordinate set off the predominant voice.

A good cadenza is usually to be conceived as embellished melody, and not etudewise as a mere interruption of the main flow to allow for a show of manual dexterity. Important it is to engage the pedal from the first, in its study, unless the unpedalled tone is indicated. A cadenza being by nature "free" and ornamental (its freedom is, like all freedoms, limited to its function, and responsible to it), it naturally presupposes an elegant rubato, and a rounded execution. The pedalling of a rising passage is different from that of a falling passage —the one leaving in its wake, so to speak, a trail of sound-vapor, the other plunging through it. The contour of a piano cadenza can be a wonderful thing, and is quite beyond any orchestral imitation.

Cadenzas were originally improvised, then they were studiedly improvised (that is, with aid of sketches), and at last they were writtenly studied. But their improvisational nature should never be lost sight of. It need hardly be added that, even in the cadenza, the effect of great freedom comes through the most disciplined preparation.

# Of
# Form and Style

*Music is the art in which form and matter are always one, the art whose subject cannot be separated from the method of its expression . . . the condition to which all the other arts are aspiring.*
E. A. POE

As to musical forms, a listener can easily savor music without knowing anything about them. Even a performer can do well with a sonata, knowing little of its structure (just as a painter need not know anatomy to portray the human figure). One need know little of stresses and materials to appreciate the design of a bridge. However, the bridge-builder himself, the moment he attempts to span more than a creek, must know something of engineering and its mathematics.

The formal engineering of music is basically not complex; indeed it is so simple that it often escapes or discourages attention because of its obviousness. It involves little more than repetition, contrast, variation, extention, fragmentation, combination and a compounding of these. Nevertheless the simple basic *plan* of all music allows for limitless development and a complexity which would appear to baffle memorization, were there not in it some guiding thread of purpose, some hidden "emotional science" as Gershwin called it. One could almost say that *the simpler the basis, the more complex can be the structure it will bear.* Visitors to the California Sierras are often surprised that the giant sequoia grows from the smallest of cones, no bigger than a large cherry. The right angle is at the root of the Empire State Building. The multiple, two, is at the root of all music's time values, the division of the string by 2, 3, 4, 5, 6, etc. is at the root of all pitch and harmony.

Yet, a principle of beauty there is, that escapes every theory and esthetic; and the more compelling this is, the more "inevitable" seems to us the work. "Could anyone show me a bar in the *Eroica*—a long symphony—that could be called superfluous?" remarked Tschaikovsky, himself no mean fashioner of "inevitable" music.

The writer of music has no escape from form. All the fantasies and the impromptus that have essayed "freedom" from the usual patterns have without exception fallen into some recognizable design seldom deviating far from these patterns. But the seeming futility of formal emancipation bespeaks also the inexhaustibility and flexibility of the known forms. Men change their dress with infinite variations, but the body's requirements remain, and we continue to clothe two arms and legs and a head attached to the trunk. Pants, skirt, or loincloth is about all the formal variety the body allows from the waist down. A composer, if he devises a suit totally foreign to all men's knowledge and acquaintance, must be prepared to be misunderstood or ridiculed, or else to defend it. Certainly, the weather, the climate, the use, the place, the customs, and his own position in society will all affect his choice.

Quite often he may begin in one form, and find it necessary to change to another. Then too, he may stumble along blindly, not knowing his form at all, not even caring perhaps, and discover it only toward the end of his labors. He may even purposely resist all formal learning in the hope of preserving intact some native impulse, of keeping it free of convention. Of such a one, Debussy said: "Never has a more refined sensibility been conveyed by such simple means. It is like the art of an enquiring savage discovering music step by step through his emotions." He was speaking of Moussorgsky. Of Walt Whitman, the same could have been said. Nevertheless, Moussorgsky, eschewing all sonatas and the like, found himself happily and firmly bound in a compelling form the moment he began work on *Boris Godunov*. Pushkin's play, however much he altered it to suit the music, became his grand design. Then, too, while Moussorgsky resisted all formal training, he was nonetheless a skillful pianist, through which he instinctively learned more about classical forms than he perhaps even knew.

Much nonsense is said about "good" and "bad" form. A *form is good if it serves its purpose,* if it awakens and keeps alive interest, if it proportions its materials, shapes them to the contours of human psychology; if it satisfies the expectations it arouses, even to the point of surprise. Schumann is one of the maligned formalists. The maligners fail to see that he was one of the most original formal thinkers of his century, creating something as close to epigram, apothegm, and fable as we have anywhere in music. And on a larger scale, could any work be more ideally proportioned and framed than his C Major Fantasy for piano? I doubt if Haydn would feel very flattered to know that his chief fame rests on the "invention" (call it that if you like) of the form, "sonata." An artist likes to be known by his art, and *he would far rather see it loved than admired for its ingenuity.* Of course, not the least of Haydn's charm is the mould he has cast his music into, which happens often to be the sonata. Of Chopin, it is said that his piano sonatas are not true sonatas, and are justified only by what he put into them. Could there be any better justification? How many, since those of Beethoven can stand beside them?

I have never encountered any player of talent, nor listener of good perception, who quarreled with the design of the piano works of Schumann or Chopin, *unless he was instructed to.* Trace back all such unsettling criticism, and it will be found to emanate from persons who not only cannot write a single phrase of music anyone would wish to hear, but whose very listening is little more than a substantiation of preconceived or acquired theory. It is a great mischief that innocent enthusiasm should be tarnished at the outset in our schools with a species of learning born of such an inversion of values, wherein "theory outstrips performance," in Leonardo's words. People should be allowed to make their own discoveries in art and in taste, *through labors of love;* and not be initiated into the realm of beauty through the prejudgment born of satiety, frustration and verbosity.

People speak of a "Bach style" and a "Mozart style" as if these large creators had not the universality to have developed almost as many styles as they did works. If it is personality we mean, then each author can usually be recognized in the smallest fragment of his work. We can perhaps add, too, that every great master may have seemed to excell all others in some particular quality. We can say that Mozart excelled in grace, Beethoven in the heroic, Bach in majesty, Handel in splendor, Wagner in the sensuous, Brahms in a rich and sentimental masculinity, Chopin in the poignant, Palestrina in the seraphic, Prokofiev in the sadistic. But not a single one of these qualities cannot be found in most of these composers in some measure somewhere, and the difference is more one of emphasis than of magnitude in single achievement. There are more moods and styles than we can name. We learn in in naming, *but we cease learning further until we again un-name.*

In time every artist gets to know the size of the canvas he can essay. *It is easier to achieve perfect proportion in the small than in the large.* From the moderate mean, the artist's disposition tends either toward intensity or extensity. But the extensive without some of the intensive falls short no less than the intensive without something of the extensive. The daring to do works of the dimension of the Sistine ceiling, the *Ring,* the *Ninth Symphony,* the *St. Matthew Passion* or Goethe's *Faust* is beyond ordinary comprehension. Perhaps even their authors looked back on them and wondered where they had gained the stamina to complete them, and indeed they may have been drawn into such vast orbits piecemeal, and not through a single impulse.

Simple it is to make a large outline, but to fill it is quite another matter. In works as large as these, it would be as easy to find fault as it would be gratuitous. Magellan committed the worst "breach of form" in getting himself murdered before finishing his circling of the world. Contrarily, it is precisely in Schumann and Chopin that we discover *the large suggested in the small;* and we can admire their skill in containment, no less than others' skill in development.

Of all the commoner forms, the variation may prove the most difficult for sustaining the listener's interest on a larger scale. Interruption and variety, the variation's very characteristics, are its perils no less. Beethoven almost invariably relieved the tedium of tonality by inserting a group of variations in a contrasting key somewhere in the middle of a set, creating thereby an extended triple design, often adding an extensive coda. Also he permitted himself extensions and developments of occasional variations, which relieved their monotony of dimension. The older masters seldom give us such tonality relief (Byrd, Gibbons, Purcell, Handel, Bach), and even Schumann and Brahms in some of their finest writings strain our present tonality tolerance.

The player can overcome these vulnerable aspects of the form by a combination of unity and variety: the unity achieved, wherever possible, by a continuous and only slightly interrupted or varied tempo; the variety achieved through every contrast which the form and the tempo will allow. In variations as compact as the chaconne or passacaglia there should be no slowing or interruption whatever within the steady arch of the greatest allowable groupings. *The cumulative effect of a long unvaried tempo,* made interesting solely through the multiformity of its details can be as impressive as in the grandest of fugues.

The vocal fugue is normally four-voiced, being formed on the rough division of the voices of men and women, an octave apart, into high and low. Its offspring, *the instrumental fugue,* while it continues the four- and even five-voiced tradition, is usually happiest in three voices. To keep four voices going in any but a slow tempo, with each acting out its own line of "independence" (a better word would be dependence), all with but two hands, and under the control of one mind, poses difficulties. Three voices are easiest to handle, while still keeping alive a reasonably full harmony, and indeed can be made to seem like four or even five voices through the use of additional gratuitous entries. The good fugeur, when he uses more than three voices, usually drops out one or two at a time to facilitate playing, and to avoid thickness. Brahms achieved a unique brilliance in his Fugue to the Handel variations with four voices by allowing them, much of the time, to double in parallel thirds and sixths, employing, in essence, little more than an enriched two-part counterpoint—an astute concession to pianism.

The sophisticate reader must forgive a brief disgression here, allowing me for the sake of the less informed, to state simply what has been made to sound very complicated about fugues. In order to make the argument concise, I shall, despite the prevalence of the three-voiced fugue, illustrate my points, in terms of its vocal ancestor, the four-voiced fugue.

A good fugue theme is a little entity, as hard to draw well as a human face. Yet with all its subtleties it will be found mostly (I am speaking of the classical fugue) *to suggest an incipient simple harmonic cadence,* I IV V I. No one would presume the brutality of actually playing such chords under a fugue theme, save by way of illustrating their impropriety. Nevertheless, with the exception of the few that modulate, every theme of Bach's "Forty-Eight" permits and suggests this cadence.

The voices usually enter one by one. Since they approximate the human voices in register they will be spaced more or less in the relation as shown in Example 1. They may enter in any succession, but are more likely to enter at first *adjacently,* thus providing the usual

"answer" in the dominant to the first statement in the tonic (or sometimes the reverse).

EXAMPLE I

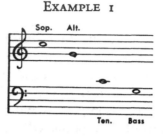

The dominant answer is sometimes literal (real) and sometimes
slightly altered (tonal). The latter alteration is made so as not to
jerk the music too abruptly from tonic into dominant. With a theme
that has a marked I–V, or V–I opening, the literal or "real" answer
would become V–II, or II–V, to avoid which, the answer is modified
into V–I or I–V, but otherwise remains as nearly as possible an imitation of the first statement. This is the whole rule of the "tonal" and
"real" answer. Understandably a theme of a more chromatic nature,
since it seldom stresses the tonic-dominant relation, rarely requires
"tonal" alteration.

Occasionally the theme itself is a *modulation* into the dominant,
and would, were it then strictly imitated in answer, send us into the
super-tonic key; to avoid which other adjustments are made.

Since it is simpler to go from I to V then back from V to I, there
is more often a *modulatory episode* between the second and the third
statement of the theme, than between the first and the second.

The first "countersubject," or counterpoint is usually the most
significant. In some fugues it has a melodic importance nearly equal to
that of the theme and plays an important role in later developments.

Other countersubjects are usually less significant as melody and
more fragmentary, and play a lesser role in later developments.

A fugal "exposition" usually means a section in which all the
voices successively take up the theme. However, some expositions have
extra entries, whereby voices repeat the theme after an interval of time.
Other expositions are incomplete in that not all the voices carry the
theme. As to how many expositions a fugue may have, it is all a matter
of dimension. Some very compact fugues appear to be one continual
"exposition," invalidating in a sense the very term. Bach mostly

changes the succession of voice entries with every exposition, giving each one a different character.

The divisions of most fugues are established by their *principal cadences*. A great number of fugues have three divisions, the first ending in a cadence into the dominant or relative key, the middle division going afield into various not-too-distantly-related tonalities, the last generally settling strongly into the tonic key, aided often by pedal notes on either V or I and stretti. With voices overlapping each other in polyphony, the cadences in fugues are seldom obvious, and sometimes deftly concealed. Continuity and homogeneity are the main thing.

No fugue is without *sequences*. Apart from their unifying trend, and the agreeable way they have of justifying nearly any pattern through rising or falling repetition, they provide one of the commonest devices of modulation. Sequence motives are, more often than not, chosen from portions of the theme, or its principal countersubject.

Common, but not essential, devices of the fugue are: inversion (sometimes of one voice, sometimes of grouped voices), augmentation, diminution (a rare device), and stretto (the theme interlocking with itself at different intervals of time and register).

In "double" or "triple" fugues (that is, having more than one theme), the first theme is usually preponderant, and a subsidiary theme bears not the contrasting relation to the main theme as in the sonata, being quite often designed to be a counterpoint to the first theme, and sometimes introduced simultaneously with it.

Beethoven, unquestionably the most significant and original fugeur since Bach (but by no means Bach's equal in fugal mastery), often used the fugal exposition alone, as fughetta or fugato, as an element of sonata development; or else he alloyed the fugue with the rondo or sonata in a larger plan; and thus effected a unique marriage between the homogeneous and the heterogeneous, or between the nondramatic and the dramatic.

It has become fashionable among scholars of late to say that the fugue is not a "form," that it is a procedure, and even a mere "texture." While it is true that there are wide deviations in the uses of, and within, fugues, they are no wider than the deviations within the sonata, the rondo, and the variation form. Certain it is that the fugue is the closest knit and most nearly formal of all the more usual forms.

# TECHNICALLY
# SPEAKING

\*

# *Of*
# *the Hands*

> *Stiffness hampers all movement, above all the con-*
> *stantly required extension and contraction of the*
> *hands.*                                    C. P. E. BACH

Since most music has in it an element of dance, it is only proper that
the members of the body which are engaged in making music should
be doing a dance of their own. Manifest or not, it is a matter of the
player's physique and personality, as well as the music's character.
Clearly, it should not call attention to itself; only that music being a
thing of grace, it deserves to be made with grace, and thus grace effaces
itself.

From the very first, a purely mechanical approach to piano playing is to be avoided, such as that the hand is merely there to depress,
pianola-like, the keys. For the hand is irregular to the point where no
two fingers are alike in strength, independence, length, leverage, or
angle. The most individual and separately independent of its members
is the thumb. Next to it in these respects is the little finger, which is
often used, like the thumb, as a digit for setting over. Next in freedom
and dexterity is the index finger, while strongest of all is the middle
finger.

The hand being wholly irregular, while the keyboard is precisely
regular, the controlling of the latter by the former calls for the subtlest
accommodation. *Weakness and strength must be equalized, or else
utilized for unequal ends.* There is no object in attempting, as some of
the older technicians did, a full equalization of the fingers in their
innate strength (as, in particular, trying to make the fourth finger as
strong as the third, or as free as the second).

From the beginning, the hand should study how to achieve a
balance between its members. It must move enough to help the fingers,
yet not so much as to impair their close tactility. The kind and degree

of movement is determined, apart from the hand's accommodation, by the music—its tempo, its dynamics and its phrasings. By and large, the hand and the arm come into use in proportion as the musical pattern is open and extended.

It is the limp hand that feels its way best into the keyboard, extends and retracts most easily, tires the least, plays the softest, leaps the lightest, looks the best, maintains a silent orientation with the least watching, and is capable of instantaneous resort to power.

A generation or two ago "weight and relaxation" were favorite topics in the piano world. They elicited Ernest Bloch's celebrated quip, "Ah yes, the pupil waits while the teacher relaxes." There is less avidity about these things today. Most pianists have come to take them for granted, yet allow that, while some very superior players play stiffly and unweightily, they still manage to make good music. A panacea for physical ease, whatever its claim, does not in the end guarantee better music. Percy Grainger once told an interviewer that he always practiced as stiffly as possible, got up all the sweat he could, and made a point of working opposing muscles *against* each other in order to develop strength. Rachmaninoff was known frequently to complain of stiffness. Great music-making is not primarily athleticism, and while performance gains freedom through relaxation, there are enough instances where such a reform would not only be wasted, but might interfere with some very desirable wrong habits.

Nevertheless, just as the teacher of singing will begin by teaching his student to relax the throat, so will the teacher of piano show his pupil at an early stage how to relax the arm and the hand, and pose *relaxation as a base from which, and toward which, all operations should proceed.*

"Weight" is merely a corollary to relaxation. It postulates that the pianist never need use downward force to produce even the most powerful sounds; that merely *allowing* the full weight of the arm on the keyboard (or in most instances the forearm) exerts enough pressure to produce the biggest tones the piano is capable of, provided the wrist is free to control pressure through its rise or fall. *Gravity gives all the power the piano will take.* Generally speaking then, the more the arm weight is *suspended,* the softer the tone; the more it is *released,* the stronger the tone. Dynamics and dexterity demand every gradation from a weightlessly suspended hand to a hand carrying the entire weight of the arm. A proper study then of "weight" in playing implies also a study of how to remove it. Striking the piano is never necessary, save as a special effect of bravura, such as the violinist uses in making a bow attack. In truth, a powerful sound made with weighty elasticity has more fullness and less stridency than any sound created through percussion.

"Relaxation" simply postulates that all muscular tensions, save those needed at the moment, should be released. Relaxation is not supineness, nor is it proper that a pianist make an exhibition of his ease of playing, beyond doing what he must to recover his ease. Music is seldom loose-jointed, apart from some of our popular music. Its tensions will unconsciously evoke physical tensions in the player. But it is possible to sublimate these and achieve a kind of tension (one could call it also pull, virility, sinewiness, firmness, meaningfulness) that is neither stiff nor supine. Carried to its doctrinaire limits, *unvaried weight playing is sodden and clumsy, while unvaried relaxation is spineless and dull.*

There is nothing so conducive to good hearing as a state of muscular relaxation. Release the effort and sharpen the ear. "The conscious practice of relaxation," says Casals, "will prove very beneficial to complete control during a concert." He goes on to say, "If you pay attention, you can notice that when we think we are in a complete state of relaxation, we can generally find some part of the body that could be relaxed more."

As between physical relaxation and musical tension there remains always some enigma. The musical tension is of course not to be sacrificed for a physical convenience. However, everyone in his experience will have noticed that *stiffness accompanies anxiety and relaxation comes with assurance.* In short, relaxation is in large measure a concomitant of mastery, and is therefore both cause and effect. Indeed a piece is not learned if it cannot be played in a relaxed state, or, shall we say, in a state wherein the hand can revert immediately after every effort, to a state of relaxation. What we are after is an effortless effort.

The principal accommodating movements of the hand and arm, while they usually do not occur separately and singly, are these:
1. The rebounding up-and-down motion of the wrist, whereby

the fingertips retain contact with, or remain near to, the key, acting as a kind of fulcrum.

2. The up-and-down motion of the hand from a more-or-less stationary wrist.

3. The lateral side-to-side motion of the wrist, whereby the fingertips turn on the keys.

4. The lateral motion of the hand from the wrist.

5. The in-and-out motion of the hand and arm.

6. The rotation of the hand and forearm from the elbow.

7. The carrying of the hand over vertically straightened fingers, like an axle carried on rimless spokes.

The cultivation of each of these freedoms calls for exaggeration in the beginning.

1. The freedom to *rebound with an undulating wrist* is perhaps the most basic of hand movements. Single or double notes, octaves or chords, are played with either a falling or a rising movement. The two attacks approximate the down and up bow of the stringed instruments. In both, the fingertips remain on or near the keys. Enough power is gained from either to produce the largest fortissimo, and there is enough yield, likewise, to produce the softest pianissimo—all depending on the amount of arm weight carried by the wrist, and the *abruptness of its motion.* Upon the yield of the wrist will depend the length and character of the tone. The tones produced by a deep rebound, sometimes called the *portato,* approximate the long detached tones of the strings with separate full bows. A sharper rebound produces a sharper staccato tone. The upward swing of the wrist simulates the upbow. It is especially appropriate for syncopations and bears a certain similarity to the lift of the conductor's baton. One may also play a legato with this wrist rebound, keeping the fingertips the while on the keyboard. The most powerful sustained passages are possible in this way, involving the forearm weight on each note. As the tempo of this rebound is increased the amplitude of motion will correspondingly decrease, and the amount of arm weight will be diminished. Quite naturally, in very fast passages the rebound becomes negligible.

2. *Rapping the keys* from the wrist (which, while being the fulcrum, need not therefore be kept stationary) is appropriate for light staccatos, and approximates in character the bouncing bow of the strings. It allows for considerable rapidity, and as it becomes faster, is reduced and becomes almost indistinguishable from 1. Naturally it is

applicable to single notes as well as to all types of chords and octaves.

3. The *side-to-side motion of the wrist* accommodates the hand in the playing of open positions of extended chords. It calls for flatness of the hand and fingers, especially on the black keys.

4. The *lateral motion of the hand* from out the wrist has a limited application, apart from its use in combination with 2 and 6. In very wide skips the hand raps the notes at either extremity, half bouncingly, as effortlessly as possible, and with the palm of the hand virtually brushing the white keys.

5. The *in-and-out motion of the hand* is to adjust the different finger-lengths to the limited depth of the keyboard. The middle finger of most people is two to three inches longer than the thumb, and a good inch or more longer than the little finger. In the playing of open passages the freedom to move in and out is conducive to rhythmic evenness, and allows for more rapidity than the turning of the hand. Obviously the thumb must not hang onto its keys but allow itself rather to slide off and onto the keyboard.

6. The *rotation of the hand* from the elbow is the commonest way of playing rapid alternations of high and low notes within the span of the hand, for example, tremulos, anywhere from a tenth down to, and including, the ordinary trill.

7. The *carrying of the high wrist* with extended fingers has a limited application, and is more often used as an exercise to develop a feeling of balance from finger to finger in the carrying of arm weight. However it prepares the hand for those unyielding, poking, straight-finger attacks which can produce the most piercing and strident sounds, suggesting most nearly the orchestra's brass.

This analysis of motions of the hand and arm does not imply that any one excludes the others. Clearly these motions are possible in every combination. Hands are either wide or narrow, long or short, large or small, and each will find a different measure of use of these various manual freedoms. Long and large hands tend to move less, while short and small hands find it helpful to maneuver more. Large people seldom use the upper arm beyond the necessary minimum, while small people avail themselves more of the use of the entire arm. Small and plump people are frequently more relaxed than large or slender people.

In general the hand tends to tilt outwardly, rather than inwardly. At no time should the player require his hand to remain precisely level (as in the old carry-a-penny school). Nor need the fingers depress the keys vertically at all times. The extension of the hand, together with its outward tilt in large spans, makes it necessary to depress some keys obliquely. Let the hand always find its easiest position, which will vary to some degree with every chord; and that will be its proper position. *Since the keyboard will not accommodate to the hand, the hand will have to accommodate to the keyboard.*

Guy Maier used to have a pretty term for what is withal an important technical gesture. He spoke of "petting the kitty," by which was meant a sliding off from the keys as a result of gathering the hand from lying flat on the keys into a bunched position. It gives the feeling of producing a tone with *an upward, rather than downward gesture,* something in the manner of the string pizzicato. It is a gesture of lightness.

The reasons against playing predominantly with a high wrist are mainly these. The wrist itself has not the resiliency, when kept high, that it has in the middle position. Then too, the high wrist tends to draw the fingers together, making open positions difficult. Lastly, it emphasizes the difference in length between the fingers, and makes for un-evenness.

The high wrist is nevertheless of advantage in producing penetrating single or closely-spaced sounds. The mere rise of the wrist places the fingers in a *poking* position, from which, with scarcely any fall, they can effortlessly produce the most penetrant sounds.

The good "piano hand" belongs to the person of good musical mind. Neither the "artistic" hand (with long and slender fingers) nor the broad, chubby hand (generally favored by pianists), nor the knotty hand, is the deciding factor. To judge a hand, one would have to measure the heart and the head.

As the piano (it existed already in Bach's day) superseded the harpsichord, its growing range and power coincided with the new dimensions called for in its literature. *Open positions* of chords began to replace *close positions.* One need only to compare Chopin's first etude with Bach's first prelude of the Well-Tempered Clavier. It was Beethoven who commenced using open positions widely and discarded the prim Alberti basses. Extension meant a flattening of the hand. At the same time, range and power increased. Accents became more orchestral and dramatic. Eventually, with Brahms, the piano was treated more manually than digitally. Since his time there has been a return to a combined manual-digital approach.

The modern pianist is expected to be at home in all of the piano's idioms. He must handle, so to speak, the foils, the sabre, and the broadsword. Nevertheless, were he to learn only certain of the preludes and fugues in the Well-Tempered Clavier of Bach, a few sonatas of both Mozart and Beethoven, and the etudes of Chopin, his pianistic equipment would be such as to open virtually all doors.

# *v*

# *Of the Fingers*

*Softness of touch depends on keeping the fingers as close as possible to the keys.*     F. COUPERIN

The fingers are the point of contact with the piano. This contact should be maintained as much as possible. It is through the tactile sense, more even than through sight, that the player orients himself. The grouping of the black keys helps the hand to locate itself, and allows freedom for reading and communication with other players.

A relaxed hand, such as that of nearly any untaught child, adjusts best to the keyboard, the fingers reaching out for the black keys and curving in slightly for the white. "The exploring hand," said Daniel Gregory Mason, "is necessarily limp." The black keys, apart from their position at the inside of the keyboard, call for a relative flatness of the fingers to prevent their slipping off. The white keys invite a more vertical contact. The thumb and little finger do well to take the black keys at an oblique angle, the thumb pointing inward, the little finger outward, to prevent slipping, and also to allow for the fullest extension of the hand. Playing between the black keys is to be avoided wherever possible, especially by persons with wide, spatulate fingers. However, of necessity, when the thumb must play a black key, the hand moves so far into the keyboard that the fingers have to play between the blacks. On the white keys the thumb does best to curve slightly inward, while the little finger may remain either flat or curved, according to the hand.

The power to make tones come through depends on either *pressing* the keys from a level contact, or else *striking* them from a slightly elevated (never so much as to stiffen or claw the hand) finger position. The first is conducive to the best legato, the second to a finger staccato and leggiero. Passages whose notes lie closely together, notably scales, employ mainly finger action. Passages in which the notes are spread more widely, notably arpeggios, employ a combination of finger and hand action.

Of scales, the diatonic are the commonest, consisting of major and the two most ordinary kinds of minor, melodic and harmonic. In these, there being seven notes to the octave, the fingering invariably uses the two groups—1 2 3 and 1 2 3 4, alternately, the fifth finger being used only at the outer extremity. The principle of all fingering of scales is simply that the thumb, being short, is used on the white keys, and falls, wherever convenient, on the tonic note. Since the fourth finger is the only one occurring once only in each octave, scale fingerings can be deduced from the position of the fourth finger. Example 2 shows the major scale fingerings.

**EXAMPLE 2**

| Scale | Note of 4th Finger | | Scale | Note of 4th Finger | | Scale | Note of 4th Finger | |
|---|---|---|---|---|---|---|---|---|
| | Right Hand | Left Hand | | Right Hand | Left Hand | | Right Hand | Left Hand |
| C | b | d | E | $d^{\#}$ | $f^{\#}$ | $A^b$ | $b^b$ | $d^b$ |
| $D^b$ | $b^b$ | $g^b$ | F | $b^b$ | g or $b^b$ | A | $g^{\#}$ | b or $f^{\#}$ |
| D | $c^{\#}$ | e or $f^{\#}$ | $F^{\#}$ | $a^{\#}$ | $f^{\#}$ | $B^b$ | $b^b$ | $e^b$ |
| $E^b$ | $b^b$ | $a^b$ | G | $f^{\#}$ | a or $f^{\#}$ | B | $a^{\#}$ | $f^{\#}$ |

Sometimes when scales are played in parallel, one or two octaves apart with both hands, it may be advisable to alter the conventional fingering in the left hand, *allowing both thumbs to play at the same time,* thus making for a simultaneous movement in-and-out, of the hands. This tends to keep the hands equidistant. For example:

C major:

           R.H.   1 2 3 1 2 3 4
           L.H.   4 3 2 1 4 3 2

or, E major:

           R.H.   1 2 3 1 2 3 4
           L.H.   4 3 2 1 4 3 2

Quite often too, the left hand fingering will be altered to suit its own most advantageous grouping, regardless of the right hand, or of the usual thumb-on-the-tonic practice.

For example, D major:

L.H., 2 1 4 3 2 1 3

Diatonic scales in thirds are ordinarily fingered with a pattern,

R.H., 3 4 5 2 3 4 5
1 2 3 1–1 2 3

which is placed at the most convenient point of the scale. Sometimes ascending and descending scales in diatonic double thirds are best fingered differently. Advantage is taken of the thumb sliding off the black onto an adjacent white key. See the following examples for right hand.

B major, ascending:

3 4 5 3 4 5 2
–1 2 3 1 2 3 1–

B major, descending:

3 5 4 3 2 5 4
1 3 2 1–1 3 2

Chromatic scales in double minor thirds are best fingered by the twofold principle: that the outer part of the right hand plays 3 4 5 (or 5 4 3, descending) over the gap between each black group (i.e. d-sharp e f, and a-sharp b c), while the inner part of the hand allows the second finger to slide off the last key of each black group onto the adjacent white key (up and down, both). Thus an upward scale of minor double thirds starting on e-flat and c would be fingered, R.H.:

3 4 5 3 4 3 4 3 4 5 3 4
1 2 1 2–2 1 2 1 2 1 2–2

or, downward:

3 4 3 5 4 3 4 3 4 3 5 4
–2 1 2 1 2 1 2–2 1 2 1 2–

Any fingering for the right hand may be exactly duplicated in the left in a *symmetrically inverse pattern and motion*, provided one measures the intervals equally in each direction from either one of *the two centers of symmetry* of the chromatic scale; meaning the two points from which the black and white keys follow the same pattern in either direction. These points are d and a-flat. See Example 3. Thus e major, ascending right hand, becomes a-flat major descending, left hand. The symmetrical inversion of a major scale having *a given number* of sharps will prove to have *the same number of flats*, and vice versa. Example 4 becomes Example 5, in symmetrical inversion.

EXAMPLE 3

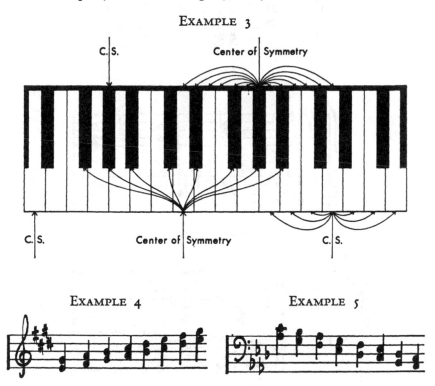

EXAMPLE 4          EXAMPLE 5

A composition can be symmetrically inverted in its entirety, not only as regards its intervals but also its keyboard patterns and fingerings. This practice would, nevertheless, have limited musical virtues to recommend it, for it would destroy the normal tonal relations. The vertical grouping of intervals in the chords would be reversed, making of normal acoustical harmony an acoustical dissonance. It should be remembered that the most harmonious distribution of chord notes spaces these in a manner approximating the overtone series, *whereby*

EXAMPLE 6

EXAMPLE 7

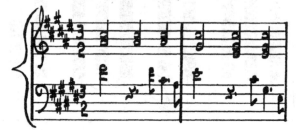

EXAMPLE 8

*the gaps between the notes decrease toward the top.* Thus Example 6 shows two chords, each symmetrically inverted.

To illustrate piano symmetrical inversion, the beginnings of two pieces are shown: the Prelude in E-flat Minor of Bach, in Example 7, and the Etude in F Minor of Chopin, in Example 8.

Example 9 shows symmetrical chords used alternately, while Example 10 shows symmetrical chords used simultaneously. (Both examples are from "Riolama" for piano and orchestra, by E. Bacon.)

EXAMPLE 9

EXAMPLE 10

Piano-symmetric inversion, apart from its usefulness in discovering the precise symmetrical counterpart, each hand from the other, offers a considerable field of speculation for the composer.

Clarity demands that successive melody tones should not normally overlap. A good method, long in use for acquiring legato scales is to *anticipate silently* each note of a scale while playing the previous one. Thus in e-flat major, the moment the third finger plays e-flat, the thumb is already silently touching f, whereas when f is played the second finger is silently touching g, etc. It is best to begin this process in a slow tempo. If the fingers are to be raised, it should be *at the moment of release,* rather than as an attack, and then only in moderation. The purpose of raising the fingers is, then, not to strike the keys, but to remove the fingers, to prevent crowding and friction.

The ideal model of an even scale is the glissando. All scale-practice should aim toward a glissando-like evenness. The hand may be allowed a discreet in-and-out movement in scales, but never to excess. A slight inward turning of the hand will ordinarily prove advantageous. Nevertheless, the hand's irregularity can never be wholly overcome, and indeed something of the individual character of each of its fingers remains as a vital factor in music, whose very conception grew out of these same manual conditions, with the composer.

It is a good study at times to practice *all* scales with a c major fingering, wherein the thumb must also play on the black keys. This calls for a limp and supple hand, and prepares the playing of sequential patterns with unchanging fingerings, at such moments where immediate adjustment to each separate scale-fingering would hinder continuity, and cause confusion. More time is often lost in changing to the best pattern, than in pursuing the pattern already established.

Light staccatos are mostly done from the wrist, in a rapping manner; but they may also be done with rapping fingers. The leggiero is executed mainly with thrown fingers, sometimes with fingers that are made to slide off the keys in contracting.

Trills in double thirds, while ordinarily fingered

$$3\ 4$$
$$1\ 2,$$

are often made easier by using alternating long and short fingers, that is to say, outer against inner fingers, thus

$$4\ 5$$
$$2\ 1$$
$$\text{or } 3\ 4$$
$$2\ 1$$
$$\text{or } 3\ 5$$
$$2\ 1.$$

It is interesting that those fingers which carry the heaviest burden of playing should be the weakest, the fifth and the fourth, inasmuch as it is the melody and the bass that mostly predominate. In order to habituate the hand to this perverse but necessary usage, it is well to practice chords holding the outer notes legato while plucking the inward notes, in the manner of a pizzicato or staccato. In time, the hands will get the habit of carrying their weight more on their outer extremities.

# *Of*
# *the Pedals*

*I know not if, save in this, such be allowed to man,
that out of three sounds he frame, not a fourth
sound, but a star.*                    R. BROWNING

Simply stated, the right pedal's principles are these: *The normal
position is with the pedal down,* whereby the vibration of the strings
is not checked. This corresponds to the normal undampened state of
the harpsichord, clavichord, harp, guitar, banjo, marimba, glockenspiel, celesta, or chimes, to cite the commonest instruments of pitched
percussion. The *upward release* is the critical moment, corresponding
with harmonic change (and is analagous to the *dampening of tone*
in the above instruments).

The pedal's depression after release depends upon how quickly the
earlier harmony has cleared.

*The time taken to clear a sound depends on its loudness and its
depth,* (that is, toward the bass). The strings require longer dampening in proportion to their length and weight.

The pedal serves two main functions, to *connect* and to *enrich,*
or, as mostly happens, to do both at once. The connection to be effected is mainly between changing harmonies. The enrichment is not
only an accumulation of all sounds struck on one pedal, but includes
the sounds due to the vibration of "sympathetic" strings.

Beyond certain elementary requirements, pedalling, like the vibrato
on a violin, becomes an individual matter. In general, harmonic passages, such as broken chords, may be pedalled more fully than melodic
passages, involving adjacent, scalewise and nonharmonic notes. Passages

in a high register permit a more continuous pedalling, that is, a disregard of harmonic change, than passages in the low register. Polyphonic music, in which harmonic change is virtually continuous, even if concealed, requires an almost constant change of pedal, or else "half-pedalling" (wherein the pedal is not fully released).

Pedalling should be introduced (children and beginners excepted) from the outset of a work's study, and not be merely added later as a separate ingredient. Playing involves the coordination of three of the body's members, the right hand, the left hand, and the right foot, and to a lesser extent a fourth member, the left foot. Such a coordination *should be made a habit* from the beginning, and it implies hearing the whole sound. As a later discipline it is often well to *depedal* so as to eliminate as far as possible the music's coloristic and emotional aspects, thereby allowing the entire attention to be focused on manual precision. But if the fruit is to be dehydrated, it must first be plucked ripe from the tree.

In playing music originally written for the clavichord or the harpsichord, it should be noted that these instruments had not the sustaining power of the modern piano. This was both advantage and disadvantage. They were more perfectly suitable for the playing of polyphonic music, since they could allow successive harmonies to run into each other without undue clouding, yet suffered not the dryness of the unpedalled piano. In polyphonic music the piano must artfully *compromise* between the dryness of non-pedalling and the enriching of harmony with continuous pedalling. The greatest confusion has resulted from the notion that because the Bachian clavichord had no pedal, the piano should eschew its use in the music of that time.

Inasmuch as the acoustics of an auditorium differ from those of a room, and the audience is placed at a distance from the instrument, it is possible and even generally desirable, that the piano be pedalled more richly in the hall, even to the point where the piano's sound may appear to the performer to be slightly blurred. The blurring of pedal carries not much farther in an auditorium than the scraping of the violin bow, or the inadvertent humming of a conductor. Consider the analogy with pictures, wherein design and color often require distance in order to become clear. *One pedals for the listener rather than the player.*

Contrarily, in the accompaniment of singers or solo instrumentalists, it may be necessary to reduce pedalling in a large hall, wherein
the relations of the sonorities are changed from those in a room. The
concert piano's resonance can easily overcome that of a single voice or
solo instrument, and is best kept in check by a sparing use of the pedal.

Half-pedalling is accomplished either by not releasing the pedal
fully or by releasing and depressing it more rapidly than usual, and
not awaiting a full clearing of each harmony. Half-pedalling has two
functions. The one is to accommodate harmonic change, with sufficient
rapidity that basses common to more than one harmony will not be
wholly lost. (A bass note may survive a number of quick pedal re-
leases and still be left sounding, while a high note is lost with the first
pedal release.) The other function is to enrich music wherein the
harmonic change is too rapid for distinct pedalling. The player keeps
up a continuous half-dampening, not necessarily corresponding with
any particular moments of harmonic change, but allowing a continual, moderate accumulation of overlapping harmony. Understandably, the two processes often coincide.

The "classical" admonition to the student is, "Do not pedal too
much"; as a result of which he often does not pedal at all, and is
praised for a restraint which is anything but praiseworthy, since it
only proves he is not mindful of the dryness of his sounds. Now as
between pedalling too much or too little, I greatly prefer the former,
for it at least allows the piano's normal voice to sound. *Better a slightly
blurred resonance than an unrelieved dryness.*

Most pedalling is a compromise between the different needs of the
separate elements making up conjoint sound. By and large, *pedalling
must respect the basses first of all,* the interruption of whose sonorities
may be more faulty than a slight diffuseness in the upper harmony.
But there are times when melody has first priority. Harmony is of
course the prime factor in both.

Sometimes the hands call for the extremes of pedalling and non-
pedalling, as for example a passage wherein the right hand plays sustained chords while the left plays staccato. Such counterpoints of color
occur often in music for piano four-hand, and for this reason two
pianos, if available, prove the better vehicle than one.

Most editions place the abbreviation "Ped." at each change of harmony, and put the asterisk just before the next pedal sign, making it appear that the release precedes the change of chord, and that the pedal is depressed with the new chord itself. This editorial practice must be accepted as a convention only, since it reverses the actual procedure, whereby *the pedal is released at the change of chord, and depressed afterward.*

Since the piano's normal tone is with pedal, *nonpedalling should be conceived as a special color,* intentional rather than inadvertent. Staccato, leggiero, crispness, and the imitation of various percussive instrumental sounds, notably the pizzicato or the spiccato of the strings; these are the main provinces of the nonpedalled tone. Then too, there is the alternation between it and the pedalled tone, upon which so much of phrasing depends, and the pianistic depiction of bowing, breathing, and pausing.

The middle, or sostenuto, pedal, being an American invention, has only recently come into use abroad, and as a consequence is seldom indicated in classical scores. When it is depressed, all dampers raised at the moment off the strings remain raised, regardless of subsequent use of either the right or left pedal. Its main purpose is to sustain basses through changing harmony. Many players overlook its effective use in combination with the "soft" pedal, requiring a slight twisting of the left foot, to enable it to hold down the two pedals at once, allowing at the same time a free use of the right pedal.

That the sostenuto pedal is of recent invention should not prejudice the player against using it in older music, which is quite as replete with pedal tones as is the music of today. Since it is now possible to sound a piano's pedal tone through to its natural conclusion, along with changing harmony, shall we insist on letting it sound only in the memory, just because Bach or Beethoven had not our sostenuto pedal? There is no point in pushing historical verisimilitude too far, when dealing with an instrument so far removed from the historical.

Like the vibrato with the violinist, nothing so much reveals a pianist's capacity to hear himself as his pedalling. One could almost say that pedalling *is* tone.

When all the sounds are high and soft, an unchanging pedal may produce an agreeable interlacing of harmony, as with the celesta, the glockenspiel, the marimba, the harp, or the guitar. This needs special listening, since nearly everyone has made it muscularly habitual to change pedal with changing harmony, regardless.

In the declamation of melody, the close grouping of notes, (as in turns, mordents, trills and rapid passing, neighboring or appoggiatura notes) may require *depedalling to compensate for the accumulation,* not only of *nonharmonic,* but of *many close* sounds. How much to depedal must depend on how much the sound-level is dropped during their execution.

The left, or "soft" pedal reduces on the grand piano the number of strings struck by the hammers, and thus its softening is a *reduction of sonority.* On the upright piano, the softening effect is achieved by lessening the stroke of the hammer and effecting a *reduction of impact.* In either, there is a change in the character of sound, but it is not the same change, nor is the change as marked as with the introduction of mutes in the family of strings or brasses. Thus it is that the left pedal is used more to reduce sound than to change its character.

# THE
# LEARNER

*

# *Of*
# *Study*

*Work alone will efface the footsteps of work.*
J. McNeill Whistler

Learning to play is learning to practice. Only the consummate performer fully understands the art of practice. Thus do study and achievement mount in turn on each other's shoulders along the formidable grade up Parnassus. Contrarily said, if a man's playing suffers from bad practicing, then his practicing suffers from bad playing. A chicken, said Samuel Butler, is an egg's way of making another egg.

The study of a work should begin like an oil portrait. You sketch in the main outlines; you add then certain tones perhaps; then comes the laying on of paint, the large labor; and finally there is the critical appraisal with last modifications. The important thing is to *progress from the general to the particular, returning finally to the general again.*

Begin with an over-all reading and a formulation of the work's musical qualities, tempos, climaxes, characteristics, and its general plan. Then settle down to a successive mastery of every one of its details—the plumbing, carpentry, masonry, and electrical wiring, so to speak. No need to involve the larger emotions for these lesser tasks, wherein one detail after another is laid away in memory and habit, each needing reassembling into successively larger units, thereafter. Finally play the work in its entirety, being careful not to exceed a tempo allowing for correctness and a realization of all that was intended. After that, many repetitions and, in time, with a lessening of solicitude comes a growing freedom. If then the work can be put to rest and taken up again at a later date, it will have been absorbed by the personality until author and player have become one.

Since nearly all music for the piano moves in rhythms, contained within regular beats (no different from those of the conductor), it is proper that the exercise of scales, arpeggios, and other elements of technique be compassed by these same beats. In short, *all exercises should be done in rhythm.* This not only realizes a metrical fact, but it encourages the development of an inner pulse, and exploits *the driving force of rhythm* in promoting dexterity, while encouraging the grace of the hands.

Toward this end, the metronome is less than useless. Nothing is so unrhythmic as the metronome. Rhythm is a human and not a mechanical thing. It springs from bodily movement, which is never perfectly regular, but the regularity of which is enhanced and humanized through the ever-present need and possibility of slight deviation. What could demonstrate this better than the pianola, whose timings are as lifeless as they are mechanically exact? If it has any attraction, it is that of the robot. Note values are ever an approximation. "We could almost think of music as being a perpetual rubato," remarks Casals.

Many have the futile habit of commencing practice on a work at its beginning, at every rehearsal. They forgot that any one portion of a work may need the same separate attention as any other, and deserves the benefit of a fresh approach. Starting always at the beginning usually leads to an eventual blemish or breakdown which, even if corrected, results only in *the double habit of error plus correction.* To overcome this practice, the player would do well to mark off the main sections of a work, and its subdivisions; then take up in turn each one of these portions at the beginning of successive practice sessions, mastering and even memorizing it, if possible, with no regard for other sections, for the time being. Later, the smaller sections that have been learned will be joined into larger sections; and in time these larger sections will be assembled to make up the whole. The final result *is a large habit made up of many small habits.*

The study of rapidity suggests two approaches. One can begin slowly, and then gradually increase the speed, as is commonly done. Or one can begin with the smallest manageable fragment played in full tempo; then follow with another such small fragment; presently joining these lesser fragments into a larger group; and ultimately joining the larger groups into a totality. Not to disparage the importance of slow practice, it is manifestly impossible to learn to play rapidly by playing only slowly. *Slowness gives the feel; rapidity the gesture.* By coupling ever-growing fractions of a passage in full tempo, it can be brought to a high state of perfection.

In general, *the faster a passage goes, the lighter it should be played.* Speed and loudness affect each other, not only as regards the capacities of the hands, but as they affect the quality of sound.

Continuous loudness does not require constant heavy playing; but can be produced through an accumulation of pedalled sound together with strategic accents. The ear also pedals, in that it carries sounds and sound-levels beyond their actuality. It resonates intention. *Power is an effect, and not a fact;* an impression and not simply force.

In the development of a student, fluency is usually his first ambition and accomplishment. Later there comes a sense for power and tone. Rhythm is the last to be achieved, and with it a sense for *timing.* Many go through life thinking that music is only a matter of making good and fluent sounds, and to them the notion of *saying something* never occurs. Poetry, speech, singing, declamation and eloquence have no counterpart in their pianism. Every sonata, nocturne and fugue is turned into an etude, the mastery of which does not go beyond correctness, smoothness, proper tempo, and memorization. "What is there more to say?" they may ask. And indeed there is no easy answer to one putting such a question.

The method of accenting beats in practice, to acquire steadiness, may not be amiss, but it should be supplemented by a de-accenting discipline, wherein the beat remains, but in sublimated form. The beat originally comes from the body. But singing, even in its primitive form, tends to subdue this beat in striving for smoothness of line. Music mostly combines song with the dance, therefore the beat must be modified in accordance with the flow of melody.

Interestingly, a Hindu remarked once that all Western music, including even such works as the symphonies of Haydn, seemed militant by comparison with Eastern music—had the savor of battle and conquest. A Westerner could hardly be expected to notice such a tendency in his own music, least of all in the friendly, witty, and benevolent inventions of Haydn.

Fatigue of the hands is not necessarily a sign of stiffness. It can be the result of playing too heavily or too rapidly, even in a state of relaxation. Metals, too, have a "limit of elasticity" and suffer "fatigue." A distance runner will tire the moment he goes over his cruising speed, and even a well-oiled automobile engine overheats when it is overstrained.

Like a clean score, a clean keyboard is conducive to clear musical thinking. Once accustomed to a clean keyboard, the person with sensitive fingers gains an abhorrence for keys encrusted with polished dirt and sweat. A keyboard should be as appetizing as the sounds it is meant to produce.

When Buelow observed that his technique was no better than his trills, he was saying that in the degree of sensitivity of the fingers lies the measure of preparation for performance. The trill being the narrowest of all piano figurations, it can well be used as a test of, as well as medium for, the fingers' sensitization.

Since fear can sometimes paralyze play in public, one must not only "shore up" every weak point in a work's preparation (the anticipation of or stumbling through which, is perhaps the chief reason for fear), but one should deliberately practice nonfear, forbid the intrusion of anxiety. Self-assurance can be practiced. It is the elimination of stiffness in the will.

Just as it is important to know how to play *deeply into the keys,* it is important to know how to stay on their surface. Few works call for a continued pressure or weightiness. Much playing tends *away from the keys.* The persistent down-player is as maladroit as is the persistent down-beater among conductors. Of Alfred Hertz, a conductor much given to a continuous heavy down-beat, Eugene Goossens once said, "There's the old pump-handle." Solidity is but one element in music. *Much of the dance is a gesture against gravity;* in music it is the same.

The moment you approach *technique in the musical spirit,* it will begin to yield, and its obstacles will resolve into music, in which spirit they must have been conceived. It's the difference between Sir Edmund Hillary, whose life-dream was climbing Everest, and a Sherpa porter for whom climbing is but a livelihood. The end gives wings to the means.

"Empty display," people often say of Liszt's bravura passages. Knowing what he was, the most generous of men no less than princely virtuoso, I can only surmise that he invested these with some fine magic that many living artists have either lost, or else, prompted by some culturine spirit of superiority, will not deign to recover.

Ask yourself if you do a certain passage with pleasure, and you will know whether you have, or are on the way to have, learned it. If it remains an unpleasant thing, you may think you can put it down to a shortcoming of the author's. But you can, and indeed must, *learn to like it,* if not for itself, then for what you will have done with it. How many a man you have shunned until you took courage and spoke with him, and then discovered him to be good company.

The tempo of learning is as personal as the tempo of playing which with no two persons is or need be the same. How fast can you assimilate what is to be done without losing spirit and control? Ultimately, *the quickest road is to take your time.* Not another's, but your own time. This means not only not practicing beyond your controls, but it means learning to await a certain ripening of realization, and a bodily feeling of fitness. It's like wine, which isn't improved by shaking up the bottle, but which nevertheless took plenty of hard work to produce before bottling. Put your work for a while into the cellar of the subconscious, and you may enjoy the same eventual surprises over what will seem a spontaneous perfection, as does the creative artist. (Learn to know there is no real difference between the two anyway—many composers are far less creative than some musicians who do not compose at all.)

But taking your time may not be the best course at all times. A new work wants to be, and perhaps should be, devoured whole at first. The point is not to trust to extensive honeymoons.

As to what editions to use, the answer is not simple. Some say, work only from the original unedited editions, if available; but this presupposes experience in their elucidation as regards tempo, dynamics, phrasing and fingering, the more so with works predating Beethoven. I have witnessed the widest divergence of opinion regarding, for example, the C Minor Fugue (Vol. I, Well-Tempered Clavier) of Bach, Czerny conceiving it as an allegro (doubtless reflecting Beethoven's view), and Ernest Bloch conceiving it, with some justice, as an andante sostenuto. There is no doubt that polyphonic music, which by very nature is less dramatic, less imbued with human characterization, and more inclined toward abstraction than homophonic music, allows more latitude of construction as to tempo, coloration, and character. And so, if two masters may conceive such a work of Bach quite oppositely, since Bach left no indications whatsoever, the less experienced person will surely be left to flounder in indecision.

While the making of decisions plays a large role in the growth of the personality, the cultivation of self-assurance requires authoritative help at an earlier stage. Phrasings, for example, are variously indicated by the masters. Chopin will often place an entire page of music under one bowing, signifying a legato, leaving to the player the discovery of the natural vocal convolutions within such a long arch of melody. Beethoven, contrarily, will often dismember a phrase into the small slurs characteristic of violin-bowing; and Mozart will sometimes indicate an isolated dynamic or a phrase, raising the question whether this marks *an exception to*, or *a pattern for*, the neighboring dynamics or phrases.

But editors presume too much when they incorporate in music already edited by its author, if not actual note changes, their own personal dynamics, tempos, and phrasings, even when they distinguish these from the originals with smaller type. For optional signs are impossible to ignore and prove to be as authoritative to the inexperienced as they are gratuitous to the experienced. It is a useless vanity of the virtuoso or pedagogue to believe he can transmit to posterity his readings of the classics. *Greatness shows itself in modesty toward the masters.* Tovey's editions of the Beethoven sonatas are accurate, faithful to the author, and add only a few very helpful fingerings. They are what editions should be. No one had more to say about Beethoven and yet had the wisdom to say so little.

Modern authors tend, if anything, to overedit their scores. But this too has its reason, stemming largely from orchestral practice. The skill of professional orchestra players and the cost of rehearsals make it usual that new works are today *read* rather than *learned,* necessitating the most precise and complete editing of all the parts. Only the conductor need fully know the work. There is little time for experimentation. And so the composer must be sure and lavish in his markings, and leave nothing to chance. This practice of overexplicit editing he translates then into his piano-writing, forgetting that the pianist is not merely following instructions, but creating an interpretation which requires and should allow some latitude.

Some like to begin the day's work with exercises and leave the interpretative labors to a time when they are warmed up. Others prefer to attack the music directly, leaving the exercises for a time when the mind is not so fresh. It is a question of the hands or the mind getting first choice. Some, like Kreisler, play no exercises at all, a privilege retained from early precocity.

Stridency results from an unyielding attack on the keys, as well as from an improper apportioning of the simultaneous tones within a chord. A harsh treble is often relieved by a resonant bass. Nearly all high sounds fall into some overtone relation with a deep sound, or at least with a sympathetic relative of such a sound. Thus a higher sound, unpleasant for its loudness, can become more agreeable by actually increasing the total sound through the increase or addition of a bass.

Only by the controlling of enthusiasms can they be directed toward the realization of their end. In taking up a new work, a brief initial fervor may be indulged, just enough to give the work impetus. But overindulged, this fervor quickly turns into satiety, and even revulsion. The salient lesson is patience. Watch any workman building a skyscraper. There is no haste, yet the building keeps going up, unbelievably fast. "The man who could write a work of a passion so sustained as *Tristan*," said Strauss, "must have been a man of ice."

It is a matter of fire in the heart and ice in the mind.

There is no music the learning of which does not gain by *underplaying*. Quiet sounds are heard more transparently, and can be better apportioned, than loud sounds. The ear gains as the muscles labor less. Then, too, physical effort beyond a certain point defeats the elasticity and rhythm of movement. And when it comes to performance, *it is always easier to add strength than to subtract it.*

Fingering is as much habit as any other feature in the learning of a work. Thus there should be as little change in fingering as possible—

better none at all; and this presupposes the most careful editing at the beginning. Every hand is sufficiently individual to need some altering of even the best published fingerings; moreover some editors finger so sparingly (often ignoring the difficult for the obvious), that the player is required to add fingerings of his own.

Since habit is paramount in all study, one can say that even the second-best fingering is better, if adhered to, than the best fingering introduced at a stage where it must fight the vested habit of another.

"Practice makes perfect," says the old saw, but it does not say that *practice unmakes perfection when carried too far.* When a person goes beyond his limits of concentration, he undoes rather than improves what he has already acquired. Bad habits are as persistent as good habits, and, like bad behavior among children, they cannot be cured by severity alone.

One must be ingenious with oneself, split the person between teacher and pupil, conductor and orchestra; watch the barometer of attention; know when to labor and when to relax, when to encourage and when to restrain, and to balance emotion with discipline.

Most people play too many notes. They think physical effort is accomplishment. They put in too many foot-pounds of energy. They rest too little. *They hear themselves too much through their muscles.* Let them watch an athlete at work and witness how often he rests between labors, and see how the supreme brief effort is framed in repose, self-examination and the crescendo of will.

Length of practice has no rule. Health, vitality, urgency, will all contribute to the discovery of what is the individual's best routine. Interest is best kept alive when energy is not allowed to totally spend itself at one time. Ernest Hemingway used to say he left his labors each day while he yet felt some vitality remaining. It was his way of making an investment today for tomorrow. " 'Tis the part of a wise man," says Cervantes, "to keep himself today for tomorrow." Part of the discipline of work is that of rest. Rest means not only sleep but also relaxation or distraction of any kind that takes music out of the mind. It often requires effort to undertake even that which is pleasurable and relaxing; for in a state of exhaustion *the very will to seek relief is at low ebb,* and an unhappy state of aimlessness ensues.

Siloti recommended interruption from practice every half hour.

Some people prefer longer stretches of work. But interruption will always provide a new momentum and perspective.

If music pursues you agreeably on quitting it, it is a sign you can go back to it; if unpleasantly, it is a sign you should remove yourself from it for a time.

It is well to invent different ways to practice. Routine is good until it becomes tiresome. Variety is good until it exhausts itself. Exaggeration (of which slow practice is one form) is good until it has achieved its end of hammering home some habit of precision. De-emotionalization is good until its aridity becomes more oppressive than the fulsomeness it escaped from. No one has discovered the perfect procedure of practice.

Nevertheless, in practice, as in playing, habits should be formed, whereby *it becomes easier to work than not to work,* pleasanter to finish the assignment of the moment than to leave it unfinished, more satisfactory to take one's time than to be pushing breathlessly ahead, and more rewarding to do clean work than work that is cloudy with incipient error.

Posture at the piano has no rule beyond comfort and appearance. Discomfort has a way of magnifying itself under stress of a public performance. Some prefer a bench to sit on, some a chair. The backrest of a chair should be low enough not to interfere with the movement of the shoulder blades, if the player likes to lean back during his playing. Some prefer a high seat, some a low. Ordinarily, large people will sit lower than small people. The important consideration is to have the forearm more or less level, so that the hand neither hangs nor stands too much.

Some like a bench or chair that is wide enough to allow sitting above or below the center of the keyboard during prolonged off-center passages, so as to lessen the arms' deviation from the normal perpendicular to the edge of the keyboard.

A natural position at the piano is not always achieved without some thought, just as an actor must school himself to do the simplest things on the stage simply: walking, sitting, standing. Nevertheless, his preoccupation with his task makes the pianist already half an actor, to begin with. Self-consciousness disappears with preoccupation, and yet a man should occasionally eavesdrop on his preoccupational self to correct the sins born of this very virtue.

In reading orchestral scores at the piano, the first principle is to *learn what to leave out.* A little observation will reveal where the score has duplications (most of which can be omitted), and again where essential melody and bass are to be found. A certain improvisational freedom is called for in simulating rapid passages, in order to avoid the difficulty of a literal translation of nonpianistic idioms. For example, in repeated notes, the strings produce a sound on the up, as well as the down, stroke, while the piano produces a sound only on the down stroke, making it possible for the violin to repeat notes with twice the speed of the piano. Thus, the octave tremulo as a substitution.

The hand cannot possibly encompass the range of even the simplest scores. *Approximation* and *simplification* are then the two main steps toward good score reading. Thus it is that a symphonic score may prove easier to read than a quartet score in which there is little escape from a literal reading of all four lines. It is well to commence score reading with music familiar to the ear, to develop this very improvisational and sketchy manner of playing.

Every artist knows those rare moments of ease and utter quiescence, often following sleep—moments not of exhilaration, energy, or inspiration, but of coolness and tranquility, when time could be said to mark time. These are moments in which to single out some as yet unscrutinized portion of a work—not necessarily a "difficulty"—to examine it for new depths of meaning, further revelations—to tie these new insights with the sensations of the body—to allow the genius of the work to flow into his being without hindrance or will. Of such moments, the later memory will recall, "Here, at least, I entered fully into the spirit of the work—or better, allowed the spirit to enter me." If this were achieved with every portion of a work, the performer could say, in time, "I know this work as if it were my own."

Trying too hard is like the novice who starts running up Mt. Blanc, and soon must pause in breathless exhaustion, awaiting his guide, who moves along in a steady walk, never losing his breath and talking very little. A good teacher is like this guide, experienced in all mountains, ready for the new climb as well as the old, but remaining withal a steadying influence, ready to help, but not to pamper; ready to save, but not always able to do so, respecting every mountain for its size and perils, mindful too of season and weather; always sizing up his charge for his talent as a mountaineer of music.

Practice *transitions*. The scene-changes that seem so simple at first are fraught with hidden questions. Will you go suddenly from one mood to another, or gradually? Will you linger or leap? Does one mood enter while another leaves, or is the stage cleared in between? Perhaps the composer has given you a flawless transition (Brahms seldom failed here), or perhaps he has left the matter in your hands (Beethoven often does), and couldn't be bothered with the detail, often the braver course.

Practice *parallelisms*, whether of passages in close imitation or sequence, or of passages widely spaced and transposed (as between, let us say, a second sonata subject in the dominant, and the same later in the tonic). Study *the differences in all near-similarities*, often the most confusing, the more insignificant they are; and sometimes revealing the composer's indecision rather than his invention.

Practice *pauses;* soundless moments; delays that honor a significant harmony, a surprise, a change, or a conclusion; moments of hushed silence, moments of loud silence (where great sounds reverberate in their momentum of memory). Study the pauses of speakers, wherein they gather not only their next words but our expectations. All this is music's declamatory province.

Practice *beginnings*. If the tempo is not sure in the very first bar, then it can be made so by practicing its silent anticipation. The pace is not to be picked up by the way; only improvisation allows that.

Practice *conducting your music* imaginarily. Your very gesture of preparation will reveal this habit, in that you move your hand in anticipation of the precise tempo and nature of the coming phrase. Imaginary conducting gives you distance, perspective and control, develops your reading and exercises that very imagination it requires.

Practice *self-attunement*, the automatic calling to attention all of your faculties at the moment of starting. Its effect on your listener is immediate.

Whatever liberty you take in altering a score for your own purposes (to justify its spirit by change of its letter), make sure the alteration is fixed and definite in your mind, and not a blurred double to the original. *It takes courage to make a change*, and it takes labor to erase the authority of the original.

Have no illusion that grace notes and all forms of light decoration can be approximated. The slighting or loss of but one ornamental note in a turn is clearly heard, in a proper state of concentration, by the listener and yourself. A lapse in intentness can be worse than a momentary miscarriage of aim or accuracy.

Practice *letting the hand feel out its most natural position*, different with every chord. The hands will never tame the keyboard if they have not first allowed themselves to be tamed by it. A silent anticipatory feeling of chords will develop their respective image in your mind.

Study the singing line, even where it is concealed. Not that it should be brought out unduly, for nothing is more effete than emphasizing what was clearly meant to remain concealed. *It is enough to know it.* Some polyphony is submissive; some reveals itself in mere suggestion, wherein the composer had the discretion to omit rather than include. Mozart and Schubert are full of this hidden counterpoint. Chopin, pretending to no polyphony at all, shows in his chord progressions a highly developed sense of inner voice-leading.

Once the learning of a piece is well under way, it may help to resort to *dry precision practice*, devoid of pedal, devoid of expression beyond a mere skeletal hint of what is intended—in which regularity of tempo, evenness of notes, and a perfect balance within and between the hands, are cultivated without the extremes of dynamics or tempo. This assures the hands in what they must do, and prepares the proper subordination of manual to musical considerations. One achieves better listening by attending to the physical doing, until it has learned to follow orders unpremeditatedly.

Since the body is symmetrical, all large movements that are asymmetrical require *compensation by the body* for the sake of balance. If left free and relaxed, the body will find its appropriate counterbalance to any strong asymmetrical swing of the arms from side to side, in and out, or up and down. One rides the piano like a horseman, and not like a manikin. As in conducting, if the beats be given with one arm alone, the body will want to turn at the hips to achieve balance. With the violin, too, such a movement compensates for the oblique movement of the bow arm. The body, if not stiffened, will find its proper equilibration.

Practice getting into the keys, by which is meant a certain solidity of tone, as against surface playing. An effective discipline toward this end is to practice a weighty portato in moderate or slow tempo, giving each note a separate downward impulse with the relaxed wrist. The mechanical nature of this procedure will not allow for a long span of attention, but *a sensation of evenness, balance* and firm finger contact will result, and may thereafter be translated into any desired dynamic or tempo level, with a suitable lessening or elimination of weight or motion.

In encountering what may seem an insurmountable difficulty, the player should consider that the composer's hands and arms were not unlike his own, posing similar limitations for him too. Doubtless the composer bethought himself of the difficulty at hand, and labored to simplify it as far as possible without musical sacrifice. If indeed, he purposely aimed at creating a difficulty, he surely did not then mean it to be easy. At any rate, the technical problem has yet to be invented that has not been solved: though not everyone is given to finding the answer.

With so wide a field as music offers, there is no reason why people must choose pieces that are impossibly beyond their capacities. A person should learn to know his level, and perhaps strive a little above it, so as to make progress, but not defeat himself with the unattainable.

Some difficulties which appear to be manual, have their origin in the pedalling. A bass note may not have been captured, or there may be a clouding of harmony from too fast a pedal change, or there may be an insufficient demarcation between what shall and what shall not be pedalled; or finally (and perhaps the commonest source of trouble), there may be a conflict between bass and melody. All listening is indeed very much a listening to the pedal, since the main sonorities depend upon it.

Your inability to master a passage in the tempo you have set may reveal itself to be not a physical shortcoming, but a protest against too rapid saying of something needing more deliberation. Your declamatory instinct may be rebelling against your too facile hands.

Your mind, your hands and your instrument are all a part of the musical cloth. This is one reason why piano music lends itself so poorly to translation by transcription.

Memory, like any other learning, is *a large habit made up of small habits*. Some memorize automatically, in the act of learning. Others must give it special attention. A work should be memorized when it is fresh and new. If the student waits too long, he has then the added task of *undoing his habit of non-memory*, of freeing himself of dependence on the page.

A habit of hand is of course a habit of mind. A man can sometimes learn a work without playing it, imagining both its sound and *its feel to the hands*. But few will tax themselves with such an austerity. A pianist likes the feel no less than the sound of music. It is said that Beethoven, even in his years of deafness, often played the piano, probably deriving therefrom an added stimulus to his inner imaginings. The mistake in always playing—and never just thinking—the music, lies in the intoxication which physical effort gives, and the easy deception derived from this, whereby *the player thinks he is learning while he is only laboring*.

Whether a player has aural or visual memory, the most reliable memory often is, contrary to most advices, that of the hands. Even during those moments of utter blankness in the mind, which nearly everyone has experienced at some time, it will be noted that the hands usually continue in their habits of play.

These hand-habits make it mandatory to cultivate an unchanging fingering. Here too, a habitual second-best is always better than a half-learned best.

Arpeggiated chords can be likened to the glissando of the harp. Important it is to *feel through* all of the chord's notes with the fingers, however rapidly, rather than merely sweep through them at top speed.

Many pianists are familiar with periodic soreness and even splitting of the finger ends. It usually follows unduly long and heavy practice. A good rule to overcome this, but one demanding self-restraint, is: *the longer the practice, the lighter the play.* The pianist should cultivate the half-voice of the singer, wherewith he does everything *suggestively* rather than actually.

Some like etudes; some do not, preferring to achieve dexterity (*Fingerfertigkeit*) through studies of their own invention, or through the use of only the common basic patterns of scales, trills, arpeggios, chords, and the like. The question does not need settling, since the value of each usage depends on the use to which it is put.

The etude (barring such as those of Chopin, Liszt and Schumann, true compositions, belonging in the same category as Bach's preludes), seeks to systematize the technical patterns of the masterpieces, and thereby relieve these latter from the burden of too much exercisive use in their own acquirement. Its drawbacks are that more effort may go into its reading and learning than into the quality of what is read and learned; also that it sometimes pretends to an artistic level it does not possess, and thus is misleading (as with Stravinsky, who likes to regard Czerny as a composer of note).

The invention of studies through permutation and combination is an exercise in ingenuity as well as in hand usage. Its drawback is that, the better the ingenuity, the more does it distract from a preoccupation with manual sensation and the perfection of tone quality and regularity.

The playing of simple basic patterns, being the least interesting, permits the fullest attention to be directed toward tone, evenness, regularity, tempo, and all their varieties and combinations.

The virtue of these different methods of exercise depends, I believe, on the stage of development of the player; whether he needs broadening or deepening, extending or intensifying, acquiring or refining.

Morning is for labor, afternoon for routine, and evening for the imagination. These may vary, but experience shows that the critical and energetic faculties come soonest after rest; while the mind is dullest in mid-day; and evening is when the spirit is mellowest, and most charitable to new thoughts.

It is not given to many to judge if they can preserve today's momentum of work and pitch of enthusiasm for tomorrow, by ceasing beforetimes today. But here the pianist has it better than the composer. The pianist may still work at half steam, while the composer, apart from such labors as orchestration, has no faith in anything that is not conceived in full steam. The pianist can still do his duty by a masterpiece of which he has no doubt. But the composer is mortally tied to his It, which knows no middle ground between presence and absence. For him it is all or nothing.

# *Of*
# *Teaching*

*Men should be taught as if you taught them not,*
*And things unknown proposed as things forgot.*
ALEXANDER POPE

The superior teacher creates an intellectual climate sympathetic to the student's growth. He *invites* rather than *compels* the student to accompany him in his studies. He is pleased by the emergence of differences. He cultivates, above all, the personality of the student, not mainly by emphasis, but through discipline and containment.

It is traditional for the teacher to incline toward unselfishness, if partly because it represents the easier course. It is simpler to exhort another than himself, since the other's problems become clear through the formulation of words, while his own remain verbally undefined. By giving much to his students the teacher grows, yet, *by giving all, he risks losing himself.* There is in this a delicate line of demarcation. In losing himself wholly in others, he forfeits the authority of his own deeds, which may have a stronger influence than words. Losing this authority of deeds, in turn, he commences to rely on his superior station, and then to repeat old advices and experiences, whose truth wears off with every re-statement, and at last he discovers himself demanding routine conformance, as well as practicing it. To give much to others, then, he must guard against giving all.

One may teach by example, by explanation, and through imitation. Example places the burden of initiative on the student. Explanation is a translation from action into words—and requires of the student a re-translation into action. Imitation is the simplest process and deserves more respecting than it generally gets. Even the best talents will imitate what they admire, and form their tastes through the very selection of models to imitate. Imitation stops soon enough when the person is ready to go on his own. Originality should not be wilful; and the less it is hurried, the better it will be; good branches require good roots, whose soil is tradition. Interestingly some of the world's most original artists learned their craft through the frankest imitation.

Teaching through example presupposes a superior learner, no less than a superior teacher. To place the burden on the student is the teacher's hardest course; for to say to the student: find your own way as far as you can, requires that you too do the same, if your admonition is to hold water. This is why teachers who say the least often accomplish the most. There is no explanation like expectation.

Gratitude in teaching is best when mutual. He is commonly paid the best who has already been fully rewarded by the privilege of instructing others. It is a fair balance: the student's trust and labor as against the teacher's generous formulation of experience. "What a discovery I made one day," said Emerson, "that the more I spent the more I grew—and that in the winter in which I communicated all my results to classes, I was full of new thoughts."

The teacher's hardest lesson is to limit his explanations to the minimum. There is no teacher like an immediate objective: to fly, for the young bird; to swim, for the duckling; to be understood, for the child. A great deal of technical talk is not only worthless in achieving a technique, but is positively harmful, in that it makes the novice self-conscious about that which is best learned unstudiedly. The time to talk technique is when some of it is already there. The coach can explain to an athlete how to improve his style, but no runner was ever taught the elements of running by a coach. He learned that in his infancy. The superior teacher, therefore, will pose *musical aims* first of all to the student, and will allow him to tax himself to his own limits before interposing his technical aid.

The experienced teacher makes no fetish of originality. He understands the processes of *parentage*. The organic world recognizes no spontaneous generation. Why then should the arts insist upon it? "It is a wise tune," says Samuel Butler, "that knows its father. True," he continues, "there is a hidden mocking spirit in things which ensures that he alone can take well who can also make well, but it is not less true that he alone makes well who takes well. A man must command all the resources of his art, and of these none is greater than knowledge of what has been done by his predecessors. What, I wonder, may he take from these—how may he build himself upon them and grow out of them—if he is to make it his chief business to steer clear of them?" The proper originality to cultivate is personality; and this is seldom achieved through the conscious seeking after the new. The discovery of something new brings great happiness; but the pose of novelty is only ugly, and the air today is heavy with original quackery.

Learned books have been written on the *physical aspects* of piano playing, notably those of Matthay, Breithaupt, Ortmann, and Schultz, all of them rewarding to whomsoever is given to probing into the anatomy, physiology, neurology, and the mechanics of the arm and hand, as they affect piano technique. But while they may stimulate and satisfy "scientific" curiosity, they help the student of piano no more than would an analysis of the larynx, the lungs, the diaphragm, and the sinuses, help the singer to sing. In aiming to enlighten, too much mechanical self-knowledge mostly confuses. Piano playing will never be a science. If it were, it would cease to be an art.

A good rule is that *the teacher should introduce conscious devices only when they are needed,* just as the doctor prescribes medicines only when the body cannot take care of itself. The less mechanical awareness the better, as with the centipede who, being admired for the intricate coordination of his myriad feet, was asked by the ant to explain how each foot followed the one before, as a result of which he forgot how to move.

If an adult were required to solve every problem he is capable of solving, before coming to his teacher for answers (the usual weekly or bi-weekly lessons), his progress would be enhanced and he would grow in self-reliance. Quite naturally, such a course is not encouraged by either the school or the private teacher, both of whom depend on lesson routine, and regular remuneration. Nevertheless, *any teaching that encourages dependence and discourages self-help is bad.* Medical schools being few and hard to get into, their students are not spoon-fed, and they usually advance more rapidly than music students. The medical curriculum imposes necessity, the best of all teachers.

The subject of rhythm and meter can best be taught through a rudimentary instruction in the art of conducting. This invites observation of rhythmic and metric essentials, without manual complication. It strengthens regularity, improves the accelerative and decelerative grace of rubati, makes clear the nature of up-beats, syncopes, and all irregularities, and invites an over-all view of music's contours. It also awakens interest in orchestral and choral scores, some familiarity with which every cultured musician should have. Had I my way with students, I would teach them all conducting at an early stage.

The teacher must at times decide whether to work on a student's *weakness* or on his *strength*, whether to shore up what is insufficient, or to advance what is best, whether to tax or to declare dividends, to broaden the base or sharpen the peak, to dig in or run full speed ahead, to contain or release. In all this, he will have to consider, between such extremes (which are by no means exclusive of each other), how much dwelling on the one will develop the other.

A great deal of the best teaching is achieved by nonencouragement, even sometimes by outright obstruction. Strong talent, being often born of disagreement and dissatisfaction, will sometimes do better despite, rather than because of, its environment. Our schools are far too ready to legalize and accredit every new trend and activity devised to facilitate learning, *leaving to resistant minds no academic crimes to commit.* Every revolt is curricularly blessed, and soon school "is just a bowl of cherries." A good talent needs some sturdy rules upon which to sharpen its claws. It need hardly be added, that not all this academic accommodation is liberality; a good deal may be just good business.

The singularities of a great artist are what most quickly attract the student since they encourage his spirit of rebellion. Yet they are the very thing that is not to be imitated. They are his badge of personality, the right to which he has won by his accomplishment. Once the student has this same mastery, he too may have his singularities, and wear them with authority rather than second-handedness.

Nothing is more discouraging and even terrifying to the ambitious musical child than the Mozart story, for it implies failure by comparison, and poses an impossible and quite unnecessary goal. What worse mischief can a teacher do than try to make a child into something he is not? It is good to begin early and many great musicians were in some measure prodigies. But many there were who were not; some even (like Wagner, Tschaikovsky, Rimsky-Korsakov, Moussorgsky) not taking up music professionally until their maturity. What is proven in telling of Mozart's precosity?

If the whole story is told, it must include the sad aftermath of failure and neglect, in a society that valued the promise of the child more than the fulfillment of the adult; pampered the prodigy and paupered the master.

In my classroom, where all levels meet, I would rather instill in my amateur students love, than knowledge, of music. Left with only knowledge, they will at the end close their books and consign the course to forgetfulness. But if they have learned to love but the smallest part of the art, they are likely to pursue some phase of it the rest of their lives. I tell them their final examination is a matter purely of academic form; and that the real test will be given fifteen years hence.

Lowell Wells, one of the few great teachers of singing I have known, used to say, "If there is but a thread of beauty in a voice, I am encouraged to attempt to teach the student. But without that little thread, I can do nothing; all the tests and grades notwithstanding."

Could this be any less true in the piano? Let us assume a student has been badly taught. If he reveals not a thread of beauty because of his teaching, he should at least reveal a little of it *despite* the teaching. A talent so vulnerable that it will give up all claim to beauty for the sake of blind obedience is hardly worth reclaiming, for then there is no character; and what is talent without character?

Too much American teaching is by encouragement, too little by provocation. The art is cultivated in a kind of overheated tropical conservatory (sometimes called a conservatory of music), in which there are neither freezes nor storms. The inclement weather is left to be faced after graduation. The assumption is that the plant cannot survive a stiff breeze while growing, and that once it has grown, it is ready to face cyclones.

Twice in my student days I was "told off" by teachers. Once Franz Schmidt told a Viennese friend of mine, who fortunately then told me, that I was a "crashing amateur" (*ein arger Dilletant*). Later, Ernest Bloch turned on me one day in blazing anger at some misbegotten exercise of mine, and said, "Do you think you will ever amount to anything?" These are hard moments to weather, and words of recrimination easily come to mind, if not to the lips; but underneath, despite the pain, one feels the justice, and even the implied compliment in a remark that says, "You, for one, could be doing more than you are doing." I am all for exposing every student to some torrid or arctic weather. He can then learn the arts of survival. "Severe truth is expressed with some bitterness," said Thoreau. Nothing strong ever grew without resistance.

"There go the careless people," said A. E. Housman. I too was one of those careless people, honoring the art with more words than solid labors, thinking that introspection would lead me to know my talents, but gaining ever less satisfaction from such idle conjecture. Later than most, nearly all, people, I finally arrived at the desperate realization that I must steel myself to a discipline of thoroughness (*Gruendlichkeit*, the Germans say); leave no work unfinished; restudy all that I had learned carelessly; and do everything to the limit of my capacity. It has given me what little I have of a career almost in reverse. At sixty, I am doing what I should have done at thirty. Most people who knew me earlier during my "careless" years, have long given me up; but I haven't given myself up, and find immeasurable satisfaction now in limitless labors of self-restoration. I cannot predict the goal, but the effort makes middle-age interesting.

I cite this autobiographical detail as a possible incentive to those who, like once myself, have fallen into easy ways and become resigned to thinking there is no remedy after a certain age. Most people lose their sense of worthwhileness and then no longer try to recover it.

A man should remember how energy goes and comes in cycles, and believe in its return. Most of the time, when he thinks "he is licked," he may be only tired.

"It is never too late to begin," could be rephrased to say, "*It is always too early to give up.*"

The player who has made a late start, while he will always be aware of his handicap in not having formed habits in early childhood, may console himself in knowing that every step in his later musical learning he will the better understand, and be able to impart to others. He will have had *to learn how to learn while learning,* an experience denied the prodigy. His handicap may preclude a virtuoso career, but does not preclude a career as conductor, teacher, chamber musician, coach, accompanist, orchestral player, scholar, theorist, singer, or indeed composer.

Adults who have been prodigies are notoriously indifferent to, and sometimes even ignorant of, the processes of early learning, and seldom teach well. They have other problems to face than those of the hands and ears. They must re-establish contact with a society they have outdistanced in childhood. They must guard against premature satiety and the facile view. They must kindle new interests at an age when the normal person is just getting up speed. They must live up to the abnormal expectations born of their early accomplishment, or else suffer eclipse. They must carry the burden of mastery across the barrier of self-consciousness and puberty into maturity. They must shed a preciosity charming in the child, yet unbecoming in the adult. They must study how not to burn themselves out too soon. They begin life with a blessing which can easily become a burden. It is natural for the growing man to climb. Placed early on a high summit the prodigy must face the weary descent in order to mount a higher, if indeed there is a higher.

The proper time to begin music, then, is when it attracts you enough to begin, *when the labors entailed promise more pleasure than pain;* when trying is more satisfying than not trying. And who but yourself can measure that?

# *ix*

# *Of Schools*

*I can easier teach twenty what were good to be done than be one of the twenty to follow my own teaching.* SHAKESPEARE

Poets were never made by courses in creative writing. Nor is a composer made through courses in composition. The "creative" arts cannot properly be taught. The incentive comes from within. The colleges, with their courses, credits, and inducements in the "field of composition" (as if it were a field) are fostering an unreality which, considering the misleading effect it has on the students, borders sometimes on fraud.

If a man aspires to write music, the school can help make him literate; teach him the grammar of music (harmony and counterpoint), its rhetoric (the study of forms), its spelling (the orthography), its history and its literature; and it can put him on its stage as a musical actor (the performance of instruments, conducting, and singing). It can also be his impresario, helping him to realize in performance what he has written. Beyond that, it can only advise; and there is no advice equal to example. One master at work is worth a thousand rules and no end of curricula.

Of course, a student needs a teacher, and the student of writing quite as much as any other. But he should be made to understand what limitations are in store. His payment of tuition or his scholarship should not entitle him to the debilitating luxury of being spoon-fed. The school exists to supply his needs, and not to stuff him with intellectual food he has shown no appetite for. *Nothing is so indigestible as unwanted knowledge.*

Unfortunately, the schools today must shape their policies to politics and business, which measure gains in numbers and interpret democracy as the availability of higher learning to all, regardless (privately they may know that the colleges, like the army, are one of various answers to growing unemployment). And so it follows, that the superior teacher, striving for the selectivity and indeed aristocracy of talent which art finally imposes, finds his efforts undone with hordes of students clamoring, not for learning, but for anything that will admit them to social status and job security, and quite ready to submit to untold boredoms to acquire this academic union card, the degree (be it bachelor, master, or doctor). The school may try to insulate a favored teacher from its production line, but the general direction is always manifest. It is almost impossible to reconcile, under one roof, such divergent trends as between mass education and artistic or intellectual excellence.

Just to understand why music is not prospering as it should in the face of all the money spent on it in our higher academies of learning, let us consider the fate of medicine if the medical schools turned out ten times as many doctors as are needed, instead of too few. Immediately the standards would fall, through an inverse necessity. And since there couldn't possibly be ten times as much sickness, the surplus doctors would, in order to make a go of it, invent a variety of corollary activities and studies; for example, "medical appreciation," "bedside psychology," "medicology," "pedagogy of obstetrics," "statistical psychiatry," "methods and materials of pharmaceutical teaching," "public relations and the doctor," "the ethics of medical success," "the doctor as salesman," and so forth. Many a lively new topic could be envisioned, and then made requisite and profitable. The methodoctors would presently invade our public schools, fortified with curricular legislation. They would invent ingenious new featherbeddings, politely called "research." They would create a vast network of "coordination" among all these new endeavors, making countless new jobs and thus further "serve" the community. Presently, the administrator of all this great system would emerge as the supreme dignitary, beside whom the surgeon, the physiologist, and the pathologist would be the merest technical hacks.

If the student needs a teacher, the teacher needs the student, too, quite apart from the matter of livelihood. All art is in some measure teaching. The finer the instruction, the more it invites; the poorer it is, the more it compels. Work that must be forced is worth little. *Good work in art, indeed, is not work at all,* considering the pleasure it gives and promises. The only struggles worth anything in art, are the struggles the artist could not bear to be without. "I worked so hard," complains a musician. Well, in that case it were better he had not worked at all, if it was such an ordeal. Artists complain of being pursued and possessed, but their only true misery is when they are not possessed, which Wagner expressed inversely, as "wishing for the kind of health, that would make it possible for me to get rid of art—the martyrdom of my life."

An artist requires disciples. Sometimes he never meets them, but he is comforted to know they exist, for he is by very nature alone and at odds with society, whether it snubs or smothers him (there is seldom any other alternative). He wants to be understood. Praise, any praise, is good to begin with, but the more it overpraises, the more does it miss its mark, and de-compliment, compelling its subject to conceal himself in embarrassment. *Understanding is the only real praise,* for it compliments the whole man, good or bad. A teacher's great moments come when he is understood, and such understanding creates a bond of love (it may even manifest itself in the opposite) between student and teacher, without which nothing much was ever accomplished.

Coming back now to the student who aspires to compose, let him center his main activities about an instrumental mastery even to the point of virtuosity. This opens all literature to him, and allows him to know great works from within, by participation and solo performance, rather than from without, as a passive listener. A man learns more about the sonata by playing it than from all the books and the discourses in the world, just as the forms and textures of painting open up to the man who puts paint on canvas.

Of all instruments, the piano remains the best for the author, having not only the greatest literature, but because it is complete and self-sufficient. Most great composers were first-rate pianists, and some surpassed all in their day (Scarlatti, Mozart, Beethoven, Liszt, Chopin, Mendelssohn, Brahms, and Rachmaninoff). More recently, Bartok, Strauss, Prokofiev, Stravinsky, Copland, Villa-Lobos, Shostakovich, De Falla, Debussy, Ravel, Scriabine, were or are all pianists of high calibre. String instruments are good to learn for the composer, and even the voice deserves cultivation; while the organ has produced some of music's Olympians. But the example of Bloch is significant in that he, a pupil of Ysaye in violin, gave himself to diligent piano practice in his fifties and was never known to resume his fiddle-playing in later years.

Let composition then, remain a matter of inner compulsion for the student, while he disciplines himself in theory (the more rigorous and anciently rooted the better), instrumental mastery, the literature, conducting also, and general academic studies. Composing should not be made a business of assignments, grades, credits and the forced imitations which close teaching-supervision makes inevitable. *Let writing be a privilege rather than a requirement.* It cannot be both at once. If it is a privilege, it will have to prove itself; if a requirement, then it is only the school that must prove itself, and what good is there in that?

A man going into music should be told, if he aspires to be a concert artist, composer or conductor, that his true profession, in terms of his livelihood, will probably be in some field secondary to his main interest or ability. Society will engage him as a teacher, arranger, administrator, critic, scholar, orchestral player, editor, entertainer, tune-mechanic in movies or television, disk-jockey or mellifluator on the radio. The equipment for, and the inducement toward, professional music study in America is entirely out of proportion to the nation's outlet in concertizing and professional leadership. This, at least, he should be given to know.

In view of this circumstance, the serious musician may well consider following the example of some of the nation's poets and composers, such as Charles Ives, John Alden Carpenter, Wallace Stevens, William Carlos Williams; and exercise his chosen profession extra-professionally. Although this course will leave him less time for his music, it will spare him from encountering too much music under indifferent or exhausting conditions. It may be better to struggle to stay in music than to struggle to get away from too much of it. It is a question between mistress and marriage.

Dividing the study of music up into the usual curricular categories, such as harmony, counterpoint, form, orchestration, history, etc., has its good reasons. Doubtless, the fact that every one of these involves all the others implies a certain dogmatism in the separation. But dogmatism has its place in all pedagogy. In presenting a new subject, it is better to be too orderly than too inclusive. Not to separate theory into these departments could lead to a confusion more undesirable than the arbitrariness of the division.

Nevertheless I would like to see students informed from the beginning of their schooling as to what every one of their studies will be about, and given some preliminary instruction in each of them. They should know the role of each in the whole scheme.

In teaching counterpoint and harmony, I would impose the severest classical limitations. Some definite boundaries must be set in order to make headway, and the tighter they are the better. It is exactly the same as in English. One teaches grammar and not Gertrude Stein. If Fuchs' *Gradus* served such a long succession of masters as Haydn, Mozart, Beethoven, Schumann, and Brahms, its virtues cannot be wholly obsolete (although I have some reservations as to how well he understood his imaginary maestro, Palestrina).

But I would also make clear to the students that the "rules" (such as the avoidance of the tritone in melody, or of consecutive fifths in harmony) *are not principles of beauty, but rather stylistic prohibitions* belonging to a period supreme in vocal polyphony (just as was the Elizabethan an era supreme in elegant versification and declamation).

Limitation is the best school for freedom. It is the canyon's walls that cause the stream to flow fast and deep. The delta marks only the river's end. But the student should know the reasons for the discipline, and can hardly be expected to accept the nonsense about a fourth being a "dissonance," successive fifths sounding "badly," and the like. A few bars of Lassus will sooner win his cooperation in learning the grammar of that era than all the esthetic reasons you can invent.

To start a new school with vast wealth is no better than to plant a sapling in a tub of manure.

Let the school put out a few roots and branches first, and prove itself a gathering place for students and teachers interested in learning, before smothering it in money. Too much wealth is always worse than too little. With no luxury at all, and only the most necessary equipment, the good people will be attracted without false expectations. The artist's and teacher's life is mostly economically austere. Let him learn his trade in surroundings harmonious with those his career will offer him. Let his academic environment not be made an insult to his private condition.

Perhaps, as Alexander Meiklejohn said, "The colleges are still the best things we have." They are relatively free of the blight of central-ization. While there is a strong tendency toward imitation and "prec-edent" in the colleges, there is no visible compulsion of the lesser by the greater. Accreditation has a long arm, and is sometimes repressive of imaginative policies, which threaten the accepted routine; but by and large, its benefits outweigh its drawbacks. Nevertheless, despite the colleges' relative autonomy, they are doing their best to become alike; and every convention of deans and presidents is hastening that end.

Who speaks of *taste* today in our schools? I doubt if the word is used once in an academic season. The old music that was born of taste is now in highest esteem—Haydn, Mozart, Palestrina, even Chopin; yet all that is implied in this taste—manners, courtesy, bearing, ele-gance, the lady, the gentleman, respect for superiority, restraint, con-sideration, modesty—all these are somehow suspect now as redolent of romanticism, paternalism, insincerity, inequality, repression, colonial-ism, pre-Freudianism, etc. The watchwords of our time are: security (what a mockery today!), adjustment (all to the mediocre mean), grades (as if Orpheus could translate these into tones), technique (as if the Muses had become trapezists), facts (the pennies, nickels, and dimes of the arts), methods (the tricks of the trade, by whose legerde-main men are made to meet on a common mean level). *Who speaks of taste, the proper dress of truth?*

When the schools and colleges need a new man, whether as director, teacher or professor, their first thought is now, "Will he fit?" No one asks whether the institution fits or whether perhaps it might be worth-while to bring someone in worthy of some fitting-to. The perfect fit is sure to be a perfect equator of people and things, for he has presumably spent his hitherto life in the study of how to fit, rather than of the fitness of things.

Not that the superior man must wholly upset what is already there, for human beings and traditions are at the root of all institutions; but he may, and almost always should, set a new course. Indeed I know of no school of music that does not need to set a new course; but I also know of few that intend to do so. For, with vested interests, there are everywhere vested comforts, vested mediocrities, vested hierarchies, vested tyrannies, vested slaveries, vested profits, vested failures, vested excellencies, too, vested pretensions, and vested expectations.

And so it is, wherever a chair or an office is open, they look for a fit, instead of a man.

The downfall of many an academic music school happens because it recognizes no downfall even when it is down. Under the protective guise of higher learning, the inefficiencies that would cripple an industry are benignly shielded from criticism. "It's hard to kill a college," said President Ferry. Perhaps he meant, you can't kill a corpse.

"It is a splendid thing," remarked Robert Henri, the painter, "to live in the environment of great students. . . . They stir the waters." This too has changed. Today all but a handful of students in a college come either because they have nothing better to do, or to make a good marriage, or else to provide themselves with the credentials for making a living in what seems from the outside an agreeable occupation. They cannot know that the loftier the pursuit, the more it brings disappointment to those who fail or tire before times. That is why musicians, on the whole, are among the unhappiest of people.

As in the mountains, a true climber is not happy unless he can reach the summit; and unclimbed or dangerously formidable peaks become his dream. Were he to learn that mountains are no less beautiful seen from below, and that a walk up to an alm can be as rewarding as a first ascent, he might have something to fall back on, once he discovers he is no Whymper, Abruzzi, or Clyde. But our schools and teachers thrive on the false encouragement of high and unreal ambition, the while they teach on the level of potato growers. They promise the Andes and Himalayas, when they could well be encouraging mountain lovers to know, to respect, to paint, to see, to geologize, to poetize, to botanize, to walk in, to camp in, to humanize, their artistic mountains; in short, to love rather than conquer, and leave the conquering to conquerors.

The mere presence of a creative man, it is slowly being discovered, has untold value to the students of a campus, regardless of whether he officially imparts his knowledge or not. For most students, such a presence is no more than the subject for a boast or a belittlement, depending on their upbringing or perspicacity; but there will always be a few, or perhaps but one, somewhere around, whose secret feeling of dedication will be sparked by the contact, however brief. Not a word need be exchanged and there need be no *togetherness* or sociability, nor any of those official blessings of credits and grades, and the influence may not show itself for years afterward.

Nevertheless, as the Arabs say, "A fig-tree looking on a fig-tree becometh fruitful." If the school produce but one Bizet or Verdi, one Toscanini or Casals in a generation, it will have surpassed its competitors though they have stuffed libraries with dour dissertations, and populated states with doctors of musical divinity.

Education has come to be thought of as the banking of knowledge. But idle knowledge, like idle money, mostly goes bad. Many people are full of a rotting store of useless facts, having yielded to the siren exhortings of passivity the moment they are through school. For them, higher education proves to have been a mistake. If women, they should have occupied their school years learning practical arts of the household—nursing, cooking, sewing, decorating, entertaining—all highly honorable, in which American women are less adept than Siberian peasants, apart from knowing how to *buy* what others make and do. One good French or Chinese cook would be worth a dozen food chemists, economics professors and marriage counsellors in one of our college Home Economics departments. Not inconceivably, a Swiss or Austrian hotel porter would do better in teaching foreign languages than some of our doctored illiterates.

If a man, can anyone show how the study (and is it a study?) of Goethe, Spinoza, Newton, Pasteur, Gibbon, Velásquez, Haydn, Faraday, Jung, or Toynbee will better fit him to sell radios, cars, air conditioners, refrigerators, appliances, boats, power mowers and all the rest, in a world which, while growing in technology, requires an ever smaller group of men to do its thinking, and puts the rest to *selling* or the anthropo-automation of the production line? Culture can only unfit him for all this, and yield restlessness instead of relief or solace. What is gained by sharpening a tool intended for such a dull use?

It is interesting that we, who consider ourselves the most practical people, conduct the most inefficient education in the entire world in all except the sciences (in which two efficiencies are running a sort of cancelling race, the one to save life, the other to obliterate it).

Who will presume to measure the aspiration of youth? What sorry devices are those "tests and measurements" that imagine they can, as a result of a few laboratory trials in pitch and rhythm, predict a personality, his poetic sense, his tenacity, or his will. Indeed, I know of some talents who expressed their contempt for this flimsy initiation into the academic life by deliberately contriving a poor score. The very men who devised the most famous of these musical tests, Seashore and Kwalwasser, regarded them at best either as a handy tool to eliminate the totally unmusical (who would have revealed themselves quite as readily on a brief personal interview with anyone more experienced than a filing clerk), or else as a record from which to measure the variations of later progress.

Has anyone devised a test for character?

In the old apprentice system, a magister may have taken on students of indifferent talent and personality, but by and large he chose them because he liked them, or found them talented or useful. He was the one to select, and not some administrative underling intent upon filling teachers' schedules, on increasing the enrollment, or on equalizing the unequal capacities within a given academic rank.

There never was a good teacher without a good learner. Nor is any one teacher good for all talent. There must be some common ground, some point of contact between teacher and pupil, to make the bond successful. Once there is this bond, a teacher will spend himself limitlessly teaching, without any need of administrative push. But he dreads the exhaustion that follows pumping information into unwilling minds. Given such, he will protect his schedule for all he is worth.

The ideal school of music, strong in spirit as well as in the level of all its departments, has many factors preventing its realization. Indeed, I know of no such school.

Now that the universities get the largest appropriations, the conservatories (with the exception of perhaps two or three with endowments) face a difficult struggle. They can hardly compete against free schools, supported by the state, nor does the conservatory diploma or degree carry the prestige of the college degree (for no reason having to do with worth). The bachelor degree from Catgut State College will get you farther up the academic ladder today than a diploma with honors from the Paris Conservatoire.

Formerly, the private teacher did the main teaching and a school was a place to acquire the accessories (theory, history, orchestra, etc.). Today, the private teacher survives largely through the instruction of children, such is the degree-hunger among adults, spurred on by the salary ratings in our public schools where a man's talents are "evaluated" by adding up "graduate" credits.

School heads are chosen nowadays to *run* a school, rather than *lead* it. Fearing encroachment on their artistic prerogatives, most faculties (as well as trustees and higher administrators) favor such a policy. They fear a leader more for his superiority than for his mediocrity. Denied the aura of artistic leadership, however, the school's head soon acquires power through the management of its business, and presently we find him wielding artistic authority as well, despite his want of artistic credentials. This may happen through the unseen acts of omission as well as the obvious acts of commission. He may prevent what he cannot do; make himself a place by denying those of ability their opportunities. Thus it is that the original caution defeats itself.

Understandably, he will consolidate his position by surrounding himself with persons of his own stamp, and hold in check all personalities threatening his preeminence. Woodrow Wilson's famous dictum, that an American college is the shadow of its president (as distinguished from most English and Continental universities, where administration is conceived more as duty than privilege), holds even more true in music than in academic matters, since a music school's life turns as much around its choral, orchestral, and operatic activities as around its classes and curricula; and the assignment of individual teaching (nearly always, and perhaps unavoidably, a director's prerogative) can make or mar any one teacher's reputation.

"I have known a prince more than once to choose an able minister," says Swift, "but I never observed that minister to use his credit in the disposal of an employment to a person whom he thought the fittest for it."

Now and again we find a school head who will acquire a faculty of talent and reputation beside which his own would appear to be small (we cannot overlook what a gift for wisdom lies hidden in such modesty). But he is rarer even than the leader with enough stature to either fear no rivalry, or else to welcome it in a spirit of generous pride.

How is it that a people so given to the competitive view in business, sports, and politics as the Americans, should fail to understand that in the most overcrowded of all its professions, music, there will be the deadliest competition; and that artistic decisions will hinge on political considerations more than anywhere else. Loving the art, we refuse to see its unlovely aspects, and thereby only encourage them the more.

Well then, are we not voters? Do we not have parliaments in all our institutions? Cannot a faculty vote and deliberate itself out of mediocrity? It could if it wished to; but can it be expected to act against its preponderant interests? And if those have become the routine servicing of average student masses, shall it deliberately then choose a policy of selectivity which spells the unpopular and misunderstood course of shrinkage in enrollment? *Shall it risk distinction?* Or can it be expected to be so farsighted as to see that ultimately the school's distinction will benefit even its least distinguished members through the quality and quantity of students it will attract?

This is the dilemma of most music schools. They began as a need and have become a burden. The more they have become entangled with the self-perpetuating business of teaching only teachers, the less well they teach. The more smoothly they run, the less room is there for that quality of genius without which their very existence loses meaning. Equability is not music.

But the root of the mistake is to believe that a school of art does not need an artist to lead it; an artist of towering gifts, either human or in his calling. The great schools of the past had such men in command; Mendelssohn, Cherubini, Auber, Fauré, Franz Schmidt, Glazunov, Dvorak, Janacek, and many more as illustrious. Sinclair Lewis gives a discouraging picture in *Arrowsmith* of the creative scholar's failure in administration, but this is more the exception than the rule (witness in science, Millikan, Conant, Chamberlain, Compton, Jordan, to name but a few).

Certainly, if we grant that the first duty of a school's director is to acquire the best possible faculty, who, then, but one of large format, will recognize the format in another? Anybody can recognize a name, but it is a school's business not only to buy reputations, but to build them; to recognize talent for itself and not for its recognition by others. What, shall a school have it said that its talent came through despite, rather than because of, its aid? Indeed, if the genius of the past becomes its main object of study, shall it so belittle the present as to smother the living genius?

One may have reason to fear the temperament of a Brahms, but there is more reason to fear the temerity of a nobody. After all, a school of art is supposed to be in the business of art and not of business, of talent and not of bookkeeping.

A composer may have a hard decision to make in yielding up his main preoccupation with writing, in favor of a public administrative service. But if he does (and some have done it, with promise of an eventual return to private labors), one may expect from him some insight, and surely quite as good a guarantee of social acceptance as from a lesser person, considering the sacrifice. It is not bad that a man may wish to exercise power (it may be used for good no less than bad), but it is better that he first demonstrate his capacities in his own profession, before being allowed to control the profession of others.

As in politics, we expect men to grow great in office, but if they have proven their greatness without the help of office, they seem oddly to excite our suspicion. We exalt the job more than the man. We once built a government to protect the individual (as much against too much government as against encroachment from other individuals). Yet our favorite slogan goes, "The Institution is greater than you." Do we mean the college is greater than Socrates, the General Electric greater than Edison, the laboratory greater than Pasteur, the library greater than Shakespeare, the orchestra greater than Beethoven, the church greater than Jesus? Is it a matter of numbers? Or is the pyramid of command dearer to us than the *Eroica* symphony, the great invention, the supreme play, the rescue of millions from disease, the moral light of a civilization?

I shall always believe that everything centers around the person, and that the respect due other persons (which is the whole meaning of democracy) has had its sincerest and most universal expression through men of poetic, aristocratic and cultivated spirit; in short through the artists of history, whether in painting, music, politics, or science. There is nothing to be placed above a man.

Why not build a school around a man?

# THE PLAYER
# AND WRITER
*

*x*

# *Of Performance and the Public*

*The greatest respect an artist can pay to music is to give it life.*

PABLO CASALS

Performing from memory is largely a question of freedom. Ordinarily, the soloist is freer without his score, while the conductor is freer with it. The difficulty of mastering a major piano work is greater than of preparing a symphony for conducting. The player's memorization becomes an almost automatic by-product of learning. He knows his score by hand as well as by ear. For him, the printed score, which invites dependence, and requires page-turning, proves to be a hindrance. The conductor, unless he has the rare gift of visual memory whereby he retains the image of the page in mind, with all its detail, relies on his aural memory, unfortified with any manual habits beyond his baton motions, which are at best descriptive of the music, but are not music itself. And this aural memory more often than not is like his memory of a face, by virtue of which any change can be detected, but the face can still not be drawn.

It is to be doubted if more than a few of our conductors who direct without score could reproduce their scores from top to bottom at any given point, with accuracy. Happily professional orchestra players are seldom thrown by a false cue, since they enjoy the security of the printed page before them. The experienced maestro, should the proper moment for a cue escape him, can usually depend on the players to come in right, and can either appear to be preoccupied with other details at the time, or else he can watch the section needing a cue for those gestures of anticipation whereby he can then recall his cue and give it with all appearance of certainty. At any rate, while conducting from memory may be an aid to freedom for a small few, it remains an ostentatious hazard for most.

Performance from memory began about in Schumann's day, coincident with the rise of the all-out virtuoso, the large orchestra, the large auditorium, and the grand piano. Buelow not only conducted from memory, but also required his orchestra to play from memory, a feat not equalled today.

Age sometimes brings on forgetfulness. And so freedom will dictate that the veteran soloist occasionally use his music rather than suffer anxiety from possible memory loss.

A useful device for the pianist to see himself as others see him (about which none can afford to remain wholly indifferent), is to place a large mirror on a chair at some distance to his right, say, anywhere between two and five yards. This enables him not only to gain an audience view of himself, at a distance twice that between the mirror and the piano, but helps to create an illusion of self-detachment. Like the painter who can step back from his canvas to see the effect his last brush-stroke has had on the picture, the pianist sees himself in the mirror, as though he were watching someone else, and gets away from the immediacy of the keyboard.

Besides, it encourages "blind-playing," whereby the hands must orient themselves through the tactile sense alone, which vastly increases the player's assurance in concert, and allows him to gain more contact with his surroundings and his audience. Emanuel Bach had the same thing in mind when he advised, "Play memorized pieces in the dark."

The mirror may also correct a player's mannerisms. Any peculiar or eccentric gesture repeated too often (whether it be swaying, or stamping, or sky-gazing, or ostentatious flaying of the keys, or indulging in facial revery, or smelling out the keys, or staring into the audience) will, however effective and even genuine, become tiresome to watch, once it has been apprehended. A pianist is as much actor as is a conductor, but within a more limited frame. It is better to be too reserved than to be too expansive. What you have to say will be better said without overemphasis. Of course, reservation can also be overdone. The proper manner on the stage is finally that which is in accord with your own personality, the search for which goes on in the very process of its triumphal extinction.

It is interesting how the piano, singly or in twos, holds its own against the symphonic army, with all its size, power, variety, fulsomeness, and sheer expensiveness. It is true that composers who have written for the one have mostly written for the other, but then they were usually pianists to begin with. Comparing the piano with the orchestra, the one is homogeneous, the other heterogeneous (strings, woodwinds, brasses, drums, all mixed into one salad, the savoring of which depends as much on the conductor's skill in blending as on the listener's appetite for color variety, group precision and maneuver, fustian of command, and sheer loudness). But loudness no longer signifies, since the advent of electronics, whereby one commentator can outshout 100,000 cheering spectators at a football game. And color is not necessarily better in outright realization than in suggestion; while the spectacle of command and obedience need not impress more than that of single responsibility before an audience, whose disappointment is feared as much by the artist as is the wrath of a mob by one who stands apart. Nothing in the orchestra can touch the percussive whang of the piano, and only the string quartet and the string orchestra can match its tonal unity. Lastly, while the orchestra, to our ravaged and abused modern ear, often disappoints because it cannot do more, the piano delights because it can do so much.

How to prepare for a concert? Assuming that the work of preparation has been done, the performer should not concern himself over last-minute improvements, and least of all should he make any changes, which will only confuse the memory at a time when habit is his chief resource and presence of mind may suffer no new burdens. He should do everything to charge himself with nervous energy, assurance and enthusiasm. Sleep is essential to this, and particularly sleep shortly before the occasion. Inexperienced and young people often imagine their resources of energy to be limitless, and take pride in living and working a normal day before a concert; and are then distressed to find their energies spent in the middle of the event. It is better to harbor one's energies too much, and even risk the charge of self-indulgence than the contrary. For, no man's energies are unlimited.

Practice immediately before a concert is as essential to the pianist as the warm-up is to the baseball pitcher. Unfortunately, few auditoriums provide their green rooms with even rudimentary instruments. Lacking a piano, the player may (if he has not a silent keyboard) exercise his fingers on a table, animate his rhythmic sense with conducting motions, think his melodies inwardly, and even take a series of deep, yawn-inducing breaths which will help his composure, once he sits down to play.

Pre-concert practice should be just enough to bring the player to a high point of dexterity, elasticity and anticipation, but not so much as either to induce inattention, or else fully to allow paroxysms of intensity. Above all, sensitivity should be evoked, and this is better achieved by underplaying than by overplaying. The memory should not be tried for possible uncertainties unless the printed page is at hand, to lend assurance.

The performance should climax the whole process of preparation, and never be allowed to be its anticlimax. The popular superstition "good rehearsal—bad performance," is not without practical wisdom, therefore.

Forgetting or fearing in performance is mostly an evidence of incomplete preparation. Having done a thing right once or even many times does not mean that it will be right at all times. Public performance pulls at the weakest link, at the same time that it tempers the strongest link, in the chain of experience. A mishap in performance can usually be traced to some *"Schlamperei,"* some moment of "I-guess-that's-good-enoughedness." In performance anxiety is often present, if unconsciously, long before the point of danger arrives, and is not easily shaken off once the point is past.

This is the Muse's revenge for insufficient sacrifices of preparation. Memory, like plumbing, can sometimes ruin a house because of a small leak.

"The thought of a public concert always gives me a nightmare," says Casals, and adds, "I have not known any artist as tormented as I am with nerves." This statement reveals that nerves are not always due to fear of a memory slip or of accident (for surely Casals was not one to forget or to botch his lines). A man may fear that he will not rise to the level he has set himself.

A concert is like a tennis match, except that the opponent is not across the net, but in you. You are competing with your best self, as you have learned to know him in public and in private. Your best self is free of anxiety, is spontaneous, is agile with his hands, and knows the joys of a mutual rapport with his audience. Every concert is another match with this ideality, and how can a superior artist be indifferent to the outcome?

Some persons approach it with practiced ease, and others again with no less rehearsed anxiety. The common experience is that nervousness soon leaves the performer once he is under way. But that very experience, however much remembered, avails even the most experienced little, when he faces his next concert.

Indeed, it is better to be too nervous before a concert than too cool, for such coolness may be the prelude to sluggishness and a want of alacrity and intensity. The experienced player has more reason to fear nonfear than fear; but this subtle distinction only he can appreciate.

The proverbial comparison of a program with a menu is not an idle one. Neither the audience nor the player is prepared for the main dish at the outset. Few players feel thoroughly at home during their first group. Some artists prefer to warm up with sure, large sounds; others favor sensitive sounds. In either event, the opening works are best selected for their simplicity and safety, rather than their early chronology. The audience having been presently won to the artist, and the artist having won his audience, both are then ready for the main course. In time, the attention (more of the listener than of the player), will be of shorter span and it is appropriate to follow the chef-d'oeuvre with briefer and perhaps more diverting or brilliant pieces.

The interpreter is right in believing that whatever he does best his audience will like the best. People sense the artist's level, and it would be as absurd for the serious sonatist to play the role of light entertainer as would be the reverse. But the player is mistaken if he thinks that an audience has the same capacity for endurance as himself. However beautiful the music, the listener does not share the performer's interest in its inner mechanics or the excitement of his responsibility.

Quite contrary to the opinion of those who now keep the "stables" of famous artists, there is no audience incapable of appreciating the most serious of works, provided the interpreter perform it greatly. There never was an audience which needed "playing-down" to. The artist who thinks himself above his audience is mostly below it. But every man's tolerance of high and long levels is limited. Besides, there is nothing demeaning in the playing of short works, and I have sometimes wondered why orchestral programs should not adopt the solo recital's custom of concluding with a salad, and a dessert. I cannot share the general opinion that orchestras and their maestri move on a higher level than those who walk alone.

Instead of a little more daring in the public arts, we shy away from all that is unproven and uncertain, believing that immunity from trial and error is purchasable (quite the opposite of what we do in business and the exploration of natural resources). Money ought, we imagine, to buy an effortless success, but failing clumsily with the living and the local, we put our faith then in the distant and the dead, thus *threatening the classics no less with the erosion of surfeit than the moderns with the drought of neglect.*

"Painting," said Robert Henri, "is a great mystery. No one has ever learned quite how to paint. No one has ever learned quite how to see." And no one has indeed learned quite how to hear. Those with the most developed "inner ear" would probably be the first to agree. Even the Mozarts and the Bachs (who came the nearest to perfection), must have enjoyed occasional surprises when they heard what they had only imagined in writing.

Of recent performers with a sensitive ear, we may remember: Toscanini, who made his orchestra transparent from top to bottom, fastening by way of paradigm, his attention sometimes on the littlest fraction of a detail in the midst of the greatest surges of sound; Casals, whose vibrati were alone a lesson to the world of string and wind players, and singers too; Rachmaninoff, who could evoke rich tapestries and brocades of sound; Kreisler, whose personality and playing were the epitome of strong, yet easy and courtly elegance; Lotte Lehmann, whose songs had a quivering excitement like light on a rippled sea; Elizabeth Schumann, whose tones were each an Aeolian caress; Roland Hayes, listening to whom you wondered if you had ever before heard the music of words like "Louise," "Adelaide," "Little Boy," "Liebe," "Caro," "Lord"; Paderewski, who seemed to have discovered the very voice of his Steinway piano; Serkin, whose playing of the classics is a sermon on music's integrity.

These men and women heard deeply, spent a lifetime on listening to, and perfecting, their musical voice. They had the modesty to know how far they fell short of their goal. To really hear, means to hear the over-soul, the Atman, the melody of humanity. What can be at once so rewarding and enslaving?

We need great appreciators. We need them in the laity, but also in the profession. We need men of large generosity, no less than of large ability. What good is one without the other? "I greet you at the outset of a great career," wrote Emerson to Whitman after the first batch of *Leaves*, but it took a generation, or two, or three, for the literary world to catch up with Emerson's prognosis. "Hats off, gentlemen, a genius," said Schumann of Chopin, and a generation later, of Brahms. "Publish this man's works," said Brahms to Simrock, after hearing an unknown fellow from Bohemia, Dvorak. Thomas Mann says of Goethe: "His productivity is closely bound up with . . . his positive genius for admiration." No greater appreciator lived than Liszt, whose invention and generosity fathered nearly all later music: Wagner, Strauss, Cornelius, Busoni, Balakirev, Rimsky-Korsakov, Moussorgsky, Borodin, Rachmaninoff, Scriabine, Grieg, Massenet, Fauré, Bizet, Debussy, Ravel, and even some of the Spaniards and Italians. Rimsky-Korsakov, emulating Liszt, devoted years to bringing the scores of his colleagues before the public with his superb and often unjustly traduced orchestrations. Whitman had this large generosity. Likewise, more recently, Tovey, Vaughan Williams, the critic Paul Rosenfeld, and among conductors, Gabrilowitsch. Busoni gave time, money, and his art in behalf of worthy younger talent. Verdi gave his fortune to a home for aged and retired musicians.

These were or are some of the great gentlemen of the art. Their vocabulary had little room for words like profit, business, security, timeliness, public relations, "school," "dated" or "new." We need such intellectual and human "aristoi," as Jefferson would call them, men whose pride is born of humility, whose skepticism is born of faith, men of warm and expansive soul.

What a man loses in audacity, invention, and endurance, as he grows older, he gains in economy, self-knowledge and mastery. He may not experience the romance that sparked his first encounter with Chopin (whose entire output seems a tribute to woman, a tribute matched by, but wholly different from, Wagner's); but there is another romance comes to him with the perfection and the understanding of such as Chopin, and he may enjoy his sure later mastery no less than he enjoyed the early romantic impulse that began it. He may no longer quite share Chopin's sad-happinesses, but he now savors their matchless utterance.

I am not a "purist." All around me I see this zeal for every art in "pure" form, actuated no doubt by a worthy enthusiasm and a fear of corruption, but expressed in prohibitory edicts that threaten sometimes more to kill than clean. There are the chamber-music purists (mostly the string-quartet addicts who never fail to claim theirs as the highest of all musical pursuits); there are the folk-song purists (who look with suspicion at a vibrato because they once heard a song done in hog-calling style in Tennessee); there are the jazz purists (perhaps the most intolerant aficionados of all); the harpsichord purists (for whom the piano is to the harpsichord as Philip of Macedon was to Pericles); the nationalist purists (like those Spaniards who resent *Carmen*, failing to see how its genius surpasses all nativist legitimacy); the record purists (who look with undisguised contempt upon live, and therefore imperfect performances, unblest by authenticity, reputation, impeccability, and expensiveness); there are the composer-purists (who know the "Bach style" better than Bach himself, and who would now unfrock Beethoven, having suddenly "discovered" Mozart). And there are many more such.

The purists are the Puritans of art, and they wear a grim look when anyone presumes to transcribe, adapt, edit, or interpret their idols. I join them in their concern for the vulgarization of great music. But I cannot share their literal feel for what is authentic. I care only in what spirit music is made. A certain corruption is the lot of all art. The alternative is to seal or embalm it, and then you have the indisputable perfection of death, the cult of a past life, as it mostly never was.

Yet, withal, the purist snobbery is valuable too, and we owe it the preservation and protection of much that is fine. I frequently will vote with the purists, but refuse to be of their party.

"If my jaw feels right," said the singer Eileen Farrell, "then I know I will sing well." If my shoulders feel easy, I will conduct well. If my hands are sensitive, I will play well. If my mind is easy, thoughts will come.

The story goes that Villa-Lobos, when asked with whom he intended to study in Paris, declared stoutly that his purpose in coming to this great bull ring of the arts was to show his music rather than be shown how it should be made. How sensible, too, was Rivera, the painter who, after having tried every fad of the Paris of his younger days, returned then to Mexico to paint peons with all the simplicity they merited. Charles Ives had no need for Paris, nor did Mark Twain, Ambrose Bierce, Jack London or Faulkner, nor did Audubon, Winslow Homer or George Bellows. It is true sometimes that "foreign countries will make you gentler, more human, more reconciled with the world," as Beethoven said, without acting on it. But it is often true also, as Jefferson remarked, that "youth acquires a fondness for European luxury and dissipation, and a contempt for the simplicity of his own country: he returns to his own country a foreigner."

How many Americans have returned from Paris less American and yet not more French. One goes abroad to deepen one's art, not to pull up one's roots. Most artists need Europe, and then they need to de-Europe themselves. Some Europeans need America, as much as America needs them; but those we need the most, seldom come. If they do, they probably become better Americans by not trying to be too much "American."

What a delight some take in declaring an artist "dated," and with what a deadly speed the grapevine circulates this casual interdict. One cannot but suspect that the obscure take a hidden pride in joining the ranks of those great who are fallen from fame. Every god dragged into the sea raises its level, or at least provides a straw to cling to.

For me, however, no art is dated so long as it has meaning, and I take good care to see that the datedness is not in the interpreter or in me. Our sense of dimension changes with time, and the modern blood flows perhaps too swiftly to allow one to sit through *Parsifal* without impatience. But this holds for me also as regards the Passions of Bach, wherein the insistent da capo of every aria sometimes tries the patience of even the purist. Nevertheless, modern impatience does not entitle me to say Bach and Wagner are long-winded. If the tides were turned, men of former times would say we of today are pathologically short of breath and had better look to our blood pressure.

Much of what is superfluous for us today was necessary in its time. The Wagnerian harmony was not in everyone's blood as it has become of late, not through too much Wagner, but through too much imitation of him. His is not the fault for this. Men like him built works like the houses they lived in—to last, and not to be bulldozed away tomorrow.

There is also the fact that most of the world's greatest artists overproduced. In their day, which managed well without our techniques of duplication (with limited printing, no blueprinting, no photo-offset, no color printing, no taping, no records), the demand for music always exceeded the supply. Today supply vastly exceeds demand (blessed or burdened, as we are, in every library, with the entire art output of centuries), and the composer suffers from too little use and outlet.

There is no doubt that overproduction is better than underproduction for the creative artist. Not all that he does will be his best in the first instance, but he will also not lose his best moments, for he will be busy trying all the time. Today many a fine moment is lost because the artist cannot convince himself there is any need to write at all, and wastes more time fighting futility than making music.

When it was mentioned that Vivaldi had written ninety concertos for strings, Debussy is said to have corrected the estimate with the words, "No, indeed, he wrote one concerto ninety times." This is well put, but one wonders who and whose age is the butt of the quip. The moon, too, has been known to boast of cutting off the sun from the earth.

Many a writer of music imagines he can do better with his own music than the virtuoso conductor. He forgets that all music is vulnerable, and when he arrives at a questionable spot, remembering perhaps his own doubts in putting it down, he will begin to tamper with it toward improvement, unsettling his players and often lapsing into hopeless indecision; the while the interpreter, if he has the responsibility to perform the same music, *will* make it his business to see the work through, not aware of, or looking for its weaknesses, but seeking only every means to make it effective as it stands.

In the later writings of Beethoven, by way of illustration, there exist passages of a problematic kind, yet which interpreters have succeeded in making plausible and convincing. They have overridden doubt with respectful assurance; or else they have treated these sections as neutral episodes in the passage from one high moment to another, accepting them, as indeed Beethoven often invites, in a spirit of exploration rather than discovery, suggesting more wilderness than any man-made park. How well Beethoven would probably have agreed with Thoreau in saying, There is more civilization often in a swamp than in our proudest cities. He brings us back to nature in these late works.

How difficult a biography! How hard to make a logical story of a man's life to which he himself could never discover the ostinato! All the conflicting truths which an artist sheds as he goes through life, seeing things from in front and then behind the proscenium, the truths and anti-truths; how shall the teller of this story make consistent its many inconsistencies; how make a work of art out of so much non-art as takes up an artist's life? People expect a man's life to be a story and not a jungle. And so the biographer must decide between truth and art, a truth that is not accepted as art, and an art that will not weather truth. Now and then, but rarely, the biographer lets his subject, and his subject's subjects, objects, and contemporaries, tell the story, and is content modestly to speak from the wings, as does Sandburg in his tale of Lincoln; and then we have a biography. Where can we find such a one in music? We are so full of plans for the past.

Who is not weary at hearing of "the American composer?" What an admission of failure lies in that everlasting bugbear. But the failure is not in the composer so much as in his America. His land would like to be Greece, but fears it may have become Rome. And yet, America's arts and inventions have already surpassed Rome's many times over. Where she has failed, is only in learning that she is what she is. She takes too much pride in the wrong things. She is too easily seduced by the flattery of others' imitations of these, and forgets what matters.

We pamper the poet but prevent his profession. Composing is but a part of the body of music, the health of everyone of whose members determines the general health. The creator and interpreter are interdependent, and neither one deserves, nor indeed profits by, favors denied the other.

Every player knows his technical pitfalls, practices cautions before every hurdle. He tries to remember his circumspections even in performance. No performer is completely off the tightrope, and perhaps if he were, we would not cross the street to hear him. Who wants to listen to a "safe" reading of the *Appassionata?*

*The greatest freedom in playing results from the most disciplined preparation.* Edward Royce once told me he had asked two celebrated pianists about their method of study. The first declared that once he had arrived at a work's conception, he never changed it afterward. The second said his preparation consisted largely of getting the work "into his hands," and thereafter he left his interpretation to the mood of the occasion. Interestingly, as Royce observed, the latter's performance always seemed inflexible and unvaried, while the former's gave the impression of virtually a free improvisation.

# *Of*
# *Ensemble and*
# *Accompaniment*

[Of Beethoven's Septette] *Dainty abandon, sometimes as if Nature laughing on a hillside in the sunshine; serious and firm monotonies, as of winds.*
WALT WHITMAN

The art of ensemble requires the player to hear others while hearing himself, and to proportion his sounds to theirs. The experience is at first disconcerting as well as agreeable; disconcerting because of the intruding sounds of the other players, and agreeable because of their harmonious conjunction with his own.

Each player in an ensemble usually finds that such conjoint music-making spurs his energies and causes him to surpass his ordinary sight-reading and rhythmic capacities. This discovery should remind him, however, that a high level of perfection in ensemble is not therefore, as is commonly supposed, the most demanding of the instrumental arts. Instead, it is the person who plays alone, unaided, and who must fire his own enthusiasm, and bear full responsibility for maintaining a high level of interest in his listeners, who has the most difficult assignment. There are many excellent chamber musicians who would prove disappointing if heard alone, while there are but few great soloists who are not capable of ensemble playing of a high order.

There is a marked difference in tone quality between solo and ensemble, more marked even with singers than with instrumentalists; *the difference between a single tone and a blended one.* The single tone can afford to be richer in vibrato and in overtones, while the blended tone should be purer, leaner, less assertive, more perfect in intonation, and congenial in timbre.

This accounts for the generally unsatisfactory character of most operatic trios, quartets and sextets by comparison with the blended quality of a good madrigal group. The opera star mostly knows only the solo tone, and his ensembles with other equal stars give the effect of contention rather than of concordance, of a reluctant surrender of his normal ascendance rather than a happy mutuality.

As regards intonation, the violinist, cellist or violist playing with a piano will inevitably make minute, if unconscious, adjustments to the piano's tempered tuning, while these same players in an ensemble without the piano will, wherever possible, revert to pure untempered intonation. This may be one of the reasons string players are averse to the piano's inclusion.

A more important reason for this aversion, however, is the fact that in every ensemble with the piano, it is the pianist alone who has the entire score before him, and who is placed in a commanding role thereby; a role that the first violin, let us say of a string quartet, is seldom willing to yield, being used, through the predominant melody role given him in most of the older works, to expect a certain subordination from his colleagues, save in passages calling for their individual solos. By nature, all participants in chamber music should be equal, but neither the talents nor prerogatives of men are equal, and thus it is more the exception than the rule when we find a chamber ensemble in which complete equality reigns.

If the combination is one of more than two instruments—as in a trio, quartet, or quintet, with piano—the piano, very much as in a concerto, is usually conceived in balance against the remainder of the group, often alternating with it, sometimes opposing it, and again supporting it. That is to say, the piano part is not thought of as just one of three, four, or five lines. It embodies melody, harmony, rhythm, and percussion, all in equal measure to the combined remaining instruments. Thus, the pianist has the largest responsibility toward making adjustments in the quality and quantity of sound.

Each instrument of the wind and string families has its individual sonority and penetrative range. In general, wind instruments have a *carrying power* superior to the strings, and are therefore more suited for out-of-door playing. A violin may outsound a flute in a room, but in the open air the flute will outcarry the violin. As between the violin and the cello, the latter has the greater *resonance,* while the former has the greater *penetration.* Thus, the cello's resonance avails it little against an orchestra, while the violin's penetration in a high register allows it to be easily heard through the orchestra, provided it be given no competing high sounds. This may account for the rarity of successful cello concertos.

As between the violin and the piano, the resonance and power of the latter is incomparably the greater. The disparity grows with the dimension of the auditorium. The pianist can remedy this by pedalling less than normally, for it is the *accumulated*, rather than the *individual*, sound that makes the difference.

Similarly, a work like the Brahms Horn Trio, while it employs more potential sound than an ordinary trio involving the cello, is in effect less suitable for large places. For, however discreetly the horn is played and even muted, its ear-filling resonance inevitably thins out, by contrast, the violin's tone, where the combination is heard at a large distance. In a room, however, the balance of violin, horn, and piano is entirely satisfactory. It should be remembered that chamber music, by very name, was never intended for anything more than a large room or salon.

Pursuing this strain, a whole symphony orchestra playing out-of-doors is acoustically less satisfactory than a mere string orchestra, or a military band. For the winds will tend to predominate over the strings, whereas in most symphonic scores it is the strings that are meant largely to predominate. Thus the outdoor orchestra becomes, as it were, turned inside out. Even the best of amphitheatres cannot duplicate the resonance of a closed hall, for which indeed all symphonic music was conceived.

Of late, electrical amplification has attempted to remedy these disparities, but has instead introduced new distortions. Either the amplification is too obvious, or too great (causing the player to lose stature by comparison with his overblown sound), or else, as happens when the different sections of the orchestra are "picked up" in separate microphones, the proportioning of these is left to the "sound engineer," who thereby supplants the conductor in one of his most important offices, *balance*: a presumption that has earned him the name, in Professor William Fleming's words, of "dial maestro." This does not say, however, that amplification, if properly proportioned and concealed, could not be effective in oversize halls and out-of-doors.

When the piano accompanies the voice or other instruments, its own inner proportions may need changing from normal solo usage.

There is no reason to bring out an upper melody in the piano when it only duplicates what the singer or the violinist is playing. On the other hand, a melody in the piano, unsupported by any other member of an ensemble, will need more than ordinary bringing out against a group of players, than against the piano's other elements alone. If the piano's bass is the sole support for the ensemble, it will require more sonority than it would for the piano alone. Obviously the piano may permit itself a fuller resonance in a quintet with four strings than in a sonata with one violin or cello.

Since the piano's innately percussive tone is made more apparent when placed alongside the singing tones of the strings and the woodwinds, it is sometimes better to achieve emphasis through contrast than through a competition of singingness. The harpsichord, having less sustaining power than the piano, achieved this contrast effortlessly, a fact that should influence the conception of older works when played on the modern piano.

All in all, when string players play in ensemble, they immediately blend with each other, being of a family. The piano, being only a distant relative of this family, may be valued by it more for its difference than its similarity, and also for its orchestral character, all according to the music's nature.

Whatever string players may feel about the piano, its inclusion in much of the greatest of chamber works by the masters reveals that they had no aversion to the combination. The harpsichord's timbre is sometimes thought to blend better with the strings than that of the piano, but then the harpsichord has little dynamic range with which to adjust to the larger ranges of level practiced today.

For the coach who teaches a singer, and then also accompanies him in concert, it is important that he reverse his usual role from that of authority to one of subordination. If the audience gains the least hint that the musical impulse stems from the piano instead of the voice, the whole occasion suffers distortion. Indeed, the singer, however much he may have submitted to direction from his coach in rehearsal, must be encouraged to feel the greatest freedom before his public, and enjoy the assurance of an unstinting support from the piano, even should he venture to do the most unexpected things. In concert, freedom is always to be preferred to correctness.

Sight-reading is encouraged most of all through accompanying and ensemble-playing whereby the compulsion to continue playing without interruption overcomes the common habit of pausing before each new musical hurdle. There is also a spirit generated between two or more players, as in conversation, that promotes continuity and dislikes vacillation.

In the accompaniment of songs, should the piano part be too complex to read at first in its entirety, it is sometimes well to provide only a bass line (which already implies harmony), along with the melody, sketching in a few figurations, perhaps, to animate the movement, saving the full reading for a later stage, after the main elements have become familiar.

Good readers are not always good learners. Reading facility often blinds one to the need to work on that which is so nearly finished at the very start. But if reading facility is not in itself a badge of artistry, it does not follow that an artist should not make it his business to read well.

# *xii*

# *Of Authorship*

*I am for every man working upon his own material and producing only what he can find within himself, which is commonly a better stock than the owner knows it to be.*            J. SWIFT

The composer has a real obligation to restore that princely instrument, the piano, to its honored place of the past. It has been decried by many string players, who allow it as a "utility instrument" at best, or, in Emanuel Bach's words, "tolerate it only as a necessary evil in accompaniment." It has been replaced in the home by the phonograph, the television, and the radio; it has been debased in quality by all but a few manufacturers; it has been cut to size by its elephantine cousin, the symphony orchestra. But it remains the staunchest individual among instruments, the most self-sufficient, the aristocrat who walks alone.

All this nonsense about an "American style!" I have no idea what an American style or school should be. But it is possible to recognize what one cannot define. While our ancestors came mostly from Europe, our life has become very different from that of the Europeans. Why then should our art not be as different as we are? Not totally different either, for we are not totally unique. We are neither Englishmen nor Indians. But the issues in America in 1963 are not those of Vienna in 1913, nor of Paris in the 1920's, of Moscow of 1935, nor of post-Hiroshima, Rome, or Berlin. Naturally, we have an academic interest in the various art "revolutions" abroad, yet there is no need for us to endorse them with imitation and affect a direction that is not only not our own, but in whose origins we have at best had only a part at second-hand.

The more I see of the modern "nonobjective," "nonrepresenta-tional," "abstract" painting and music, the more am I convinced that it cannot endure a coexistence with normal or traditional art. It thrives on a corruption of taste, as indeed every great disease of mankind has thriven on a corruption of the general health. It fears the survival of the littlest island of tradition. Some day somebody will ask a simple question, "What for?" that may well topple the whole edifice, as the great inflation was toppled when somebody suddenly sold his spiraling stock.

What the investment of time and labor will yield you in the de-velopment or discovery of your own talent, no one can tell you, nor can you tell yourself beforehand. You cannot know your powers until you have tried them, and tried them under fire. You cannot know the formula of your personality until you have behind you some solid accomplishments. It seems a wasteful process, to have to do all that work only to find out whether it is worth even starting; to launch out without knowing your destination, let alone direction. But that is the way of things, and would you have it otherwise? If we were cer-tain of one kind of success beforehand, we would have to bargain with the equal certainty of other failures. There is no greater gamble than a man's career in an art; but even when it is achieved, who knows how successful it is to the man himself, and who can know the price? People admire the man who "knows what he wants, and goes after it." But it is more admirable to go after the unknown, though it marks you as a fool till you've found it, if ever.

Three mainsprings there are to music, each with its fulfillment or opposite: love (and hate as well); wonder (and its aftermath, dis-illusion); despair (and its amelioration, distraction). Not the least of these is despair, from the mould and manure of which the tenderest flowers of maturity often grow. Who can tell how many of the world's noblest paintings and symphonies had their mainspring, not in love (not even in tragic love), not in worship, not in revolt or indigna-tion, but in the plain, bleak discovery that there was nothing left to do but paint or compose music. Yet once started, how the weather would then change!

Good pianism is seldom found in the reduction of concerto scores. The arranger, zealous to include as much as possible, succeeds often in making the second piano part for a concerto more difficult than the solo, and in overloading the sheer piano sound. A reduction should always aim to be *pianistic,* and to be as simple and sparse as possible. Whatever elements conflict with this end should be excluded, or else added on a separate line for reference or optional inclusion. It should avoid, wherever it can, any outright duplication of the solo's notes, particularly its melodies, because of their beat-producing and ill-suited conjunction with these (a conjunction not similarly disturbing with the original orchestral timbres). In short, *an orchestral reduction should be piano music,* and not attempt to be a literal copy of what it cannot be.

In the invention of new symbols, the artist has all the more need to present the unfamiliar in some terms of familiarity. Music's older symbols, while seldom defined, are nevertheless generally understood. They have a long history, born of slow evolution as well as radical change. New symbols cannot afford to be new beyond the possibility of translation (not explanation). No art lends itself so readily to permutation and combination as music, but this does not make music mathematics, nor mathematics music. If the old symbols become too distorted through such mathematic processes, the art runs the danger of becoming a puzzle, a labyrinth, or else a fortuitous speculation. It loses its time-honored place as the vehicle of feeling beyond utterance in words, needing no passports and quotas to become at home in all the world. It is possible to reason oneself out of all human feelings and invent a Martian code of symbols. But the great artists of the past *pulled* men toward them with gestures they could understand. *They remained in tune, even while changing the tune.* This is leading; the other is apostasy.

A slump in work is like a day of bad weather. You can pass the time awaiting clear skies, or you can ignore the weather and get to work. The mark of a professional is that he chooses the latter course, even though it may end in failure. He remembers that he has succeeded in overcoming slumps before. While a state of grace cannot be commanded, it is also not enough to just await it. A man should put his house in order so that his angel will find it presentable, should he choose to make one of his unannounced visits.

Experiment in art is not "creation." It may be an avenue leading toward it, but then creativity is nothing less than the very evocation of life through art. Men make robots and computing machines in laboratories, and perhaps this is scientific creation. But such an imitation of man's thinking process, however far it may surpass in speed man's power to compute, is not thought and will not be thought until, if ever, science creates life itself. And God help us when we begin to make life as fluently as we already have learned to un-make it. But the artist, however much he may indulge himself in mechanical experimentation, should not forego his time-honored privilege of conjuring life out of sounds, colors, and words, and should not forget his mission, perhaps the most religious of all, of sustaining a faith in the worthwhileness of art and thus of life.

The generation of art remains a private matter, and its processes prefer, as do those of human generation, to remain personal until the child is born. Nothing is proof today against analysis, and so we gossip journalistically and psychologically about the various steps by which the masterpieces of the past have come to be born. But we come no nearer to the wisdom of creation than we were before—rather the contrary. The more we know, the less we feel like doing.

Picture Beethoven pursued on his country walks by his analysts and commentators, all hoping to capture his moments of rapture, and to achieve a "scoop" on his revelations. A man's song is his love, to reveal which beforetimes is like plucking green fruit. All an art asks is to be *allowed to grow;* a good soil and climate and a little weeding. It needs no hothouses nor chemicals, nor need it serve a national cause, to become in time the nation's chiefest pride.

Hearing the scholars, one would think that writing music is purely a matter of taking a series of *logical* steps, of *selecting* between this course and that, the whole process being made to seem as simple as meeting students in a classroom. But the tasks of academic routine, wherein the problems are brought before the teacher and solved on the spot (the answer lying already in the question)—how utterly unlike they are from those problems which must be invented as well as solved, where everything hangs in a fragile balance between success and utter failure and all depends on a temperature of fervor that is the very antithesis of routine.

No book is ever finished nor any symphony or song. Yet the reader or the listener, once he has taken a work to heart, will see only its perfections. The author, meanwhile, following what Thomas Mann calls "the compulsion to exquisite precision," will become ever more aware of its faults, remembering all too well where contrivance filled in for creation; and the temptation to revise will seize him. Yet there comes a time when further refinement is bought at the price of a weakening impulse. Not everyone has the wisdom to recognize this. Maynard Dixon, the painter, once said it takes two to make a picture; one to paint it, the other to shoot him before he goes on to spoil it.

Don't be too critical with your own work. The chances are, if you have put your bowels into it, if you feel it has come out right, and then set it aside (not to be viewed the next day—always the most uncharitable), and later, from a little distance of elapsed time, you look at it again, you may be agreeably astonished at what you have done. You may discover of yourself, as some poet said, "He wrought better than he knew." Our labors and our judgments have seldom the same focus.

Expansion and contraction both belong to the arts of expression. Shakespeare and Bacon were the literary antithesis of each other, the one tending toward the flower, the other toward the seed. The two are quite irreconcilable in one person (whatever the "cipher" advocates may say). In music, the developmental has been favored, but the formulative, the concise, the brief, the epigrammatic expression could well receive more attention in the future. This may indeed offer a large new field.

Pianistic writing is always more apparent to the player than to the listener. For it means writing wherein music and the hand achieve a perfect marriage. Some great music is not notably pianistic—much of Schubert's piano work, wherein subordinate figurations are often hard to subdue, or the harmony (as in his four-hand works) is excessively close in the middle register; some of Moussorgsky's writings, more careless often than clumsy; and certain of Beethoven's later polyphonic pieces, wherein he was clearly indifferent to ease of execution.

The greatest masters of the keyboard achieved mostly a wonderful fusion of music and pianism, so intimately related that it were impossible to say which came first. Some, such as Mendelssohn, Franck, and Brahms arrived at a singularly fine union of pianism with polyphony (always a hard problem, since one mind and two hands must take in many voices, each presuming a separate line of thought), sometimes realized more in suggestion than in literal fulfillment.

There are limestone caves that seem to have no end. You venture first into their known passages, then detect a hitherto undiscovered opening, which again reveals a whole new network of caves. In time you make a new map including all known explorations, and settle down, content with what you have. But another person comes along, looking for new openings where you perceived none, and in time enlarges your map, relegating your considerable findings into the large body of the past. An era lies just behind us when the dogma of the exhaustion of musical invention was current. Wagner may have had the immodesty to believe he had brought harmonic research to an end. But the exploration goes on, and there is not a chamber that may not be sounded for new openings, nor declared ultimate.

Even though chromaticism was the avenue whose "inevitable" end has so often been described as atonalism, the atonalists are the first to condemn their immediate forebears (if indeed they were forebears in anything more than a material sense: Liszt, Wagner, Strauss, Debussy, Scriabine, Ravel, Szymanowski, Stravinsky). This *deparenting* tendency is like that of America's Communists, who flouted the Socialists above all other political theorists. When the sociological deparenting began (with Samuel Butler, Freud, and Shaw), the motive was to save the offspring. But now, judging from its vehemence, the motive seems mainly to be to destroy the parent.

The "deadline" is as much a good as it is an evil. It drives a man either into production or despair. It spawned Wagner's "Kaisermarsch" and Beethoven's *Battle Symphony*, but it also brought forth *The Barber of Seville*, Mozart's overtures, and *The Mikado*. There is no predicting the fertility of even the most famous soil on which the seed of a commission will fall. Tolstoi rejected with scorn the invitation to contribute regularly to a magazine. The notion of having to say something on schedule when he might have nothing to say, revolted him. And yet artists, for whom there is seldom a middle ground between frantic activity and frustration, often profit by a command performance.

The way to new art is the sketch. The sketch is the practice session of the creator. He sharpens his imaginings through little trials and observations, which are the better and freer for their irresponsibility. No one will see them but himself, and he may never use them, nor even look at them again, being satisfied that they exercised his thought to the point where it could undertake something more substantial. But now we are more interested in the art process than in the art itself, and thus we esteem the sketch above the picture, and even the doodle becomes priceless (at least the doodle of a priceless reputation).

Many a writer of music (notice how sparingly I use the word "composer") has been frightened at the quantity and complexity of scores of his contemporaries, and made to feel his inadequacy by comparison.

Who is there to tell him it were better that he write one good song than a dozen bad symphonies, that one good hymn is more needed than—and will outlast—a dozen quartets conceived in a spirit of pure erudition or what we might call scientific noneclecticism.

Great composers give us a momentum to ride upon. They do not change direction beforetimes. They have a long breath. They love above all to send us on an extended trajectory; but to do so there must be a sturdy explosiveness to set us flying. What fine patterns for long flight are in Bach and Handel, in the allegros of Beethoven, in the etudes of Chopin, in Tschaikovsky's symphonies, in the grander arias of Verdi, or in the songs of Schubert! No fear there of boredom or repetition; no scurrying after new ideas beforetimes.

If you light on a good flying pattern, stay with it as long as you can, and forget all the penny-wise, pound-foolish, chalk-dust talk about "variety" and "logic" that emanates from those musical stockbrokers, who have not the courage of their admonitions, and who profit from their clients' losses as much as from their gains.

Brahms not an orchestrator! Schumann not a formalist! Michelangelo not a colorist! Moussorgsky not a professional! Verdi a vulgarian! Bruckner overloaded! Chopin not a contrapuntalist! Wagner amoral! Tschaikovsky hysterical! Liszt a bombast! And so on. These views are the stock in trade of college professors. The opulence of great creation always unsettles them into halting apologies of ifs and buts, nots and yets, whys and whats. Their warmest praises must, in order not to shake the ladder of lofty erudition on which they stand, be tinged with faint damns.

Keep in mind the gestation of a work, the rotation of its crop of ideas, the need of periodic fallowness. The world speaks with bated breath of *The Messiah* being written in three weeks. But what a rare three weeks those were! What Handel could put down in a frenzy of labor in so short a time, may have been preparing for many years, like some river bursting out of Missouri soil, with sources in the far-off mountains. Handel himself could not duplicate that feat. When Whistler was refused his fee for painting Lord X, and sued, the attorney for the defense, having learned that his client had sat for the painter but a few times, asked Whistler how long the picture had taken to paint. "Forty years," said Whistler. A lifetime of preparation was behind that portrait. Time is not always a measure of dimension.

Musical color by itself is nothing to brag of. Under all is *the idea,* which, more often than not is melody. Even Stravinsky has said, "I am beginning to think together with the general public, that melody should keep its place at the summit of the hierarchy of all elements which constitute music." How many artists have learned, and often late in life, that the melody-loving public is the ultimate arbiter. Wagner makes it the theme of his *Meistersinger.*

Now the fashion is fortuity, the predeterminedly accidental, the philosophico-psychological unthought, the advertent idea-lessness, the hermetical bloop. The Rohrschach Test has become lyrical, eloquent, dramatical. The Unconscious stands revealed like the emperor's new clothes. It takes a child to not see their splendor.

But just suppose the Unconscious turns out to be like the holy of holies in the Sunchildism of Butler's *Erewhon,* nothing but a sheep's turd?

What a series of fashions the painters have gone through! First it was "light," then "pure color," then "solidity," then "prismatic light," then cubistic articulation, then aperspective, then dada, then surrealism, then Marxian politics, then post-this-that-and-the-other (all but the post-alimentary), and now this nonobjectivity (as furious as any Crusade). And what remains? A few artists, great *not because of*, but *despite* all this noise and confusion; Manet, Monet, Winslow Homer, Cézanne, Van Gogh, Daumier, Rodin, Bellows, Mestrovic, Gauguin, Rivera, Orozco.

And so today we could be looking for the artist in music, not the novel orchestrator, the abstractionist, the atonalist, surrealist, electrosynthesist, fortuitist, obscurantist, obfuscatist, or formanalyst. All these represent the political parties in music. Does anyone care today whether Lincoln was a Republican or a Democrat?

If there is to be revolt in art, *let it be a revolt against more than fictive windmills.* Can anyone respect a revolution against tonality, against the Romantic period, against a Past so present today in performance?

If a composer has something to say, let him say it with works and deeds, and not with pretentious carpings against those whose measure he has yet to prove he possesses. Such righteous wrath has a political flavor, as of a man seeking office, yet unburdened with its responsibilities.

Beethoven did not charge against Haydn, Mozart or Bach. He charged against injustice to men. Moussorgsky did not charge against Liszt and Wagner; he charged against the contempt in which his native Russia was held by its musical trustees. Verdi did not charge against Beethoven and Schubert; he charged against foreign oppression in Italy. Chopin charged against Russian abuse of his homeland. Charles Ives stood up for the dignity of the New England man; he did not run down Brahms. What is so revolutionary about some new idiomatic twist of color or sound? Does its author risk his neck or his freedom for it? No, he risks only the sudden acclaim of an art dealer or music critic.

*I will honor the revolt only in proportion to its object.* Most revolts in art prove to be little more than a noisy and inexpensive self-advertisement.

All composing must walk the delicate line between variety and unity. How much does an idea bear repeating, sequencing, extending, inverting, altering? When shall another be introduced? How much shall the two conflict? Do we go by means or extremes? How much of the familiar is needed to support the unfamiliar? Musical form does not talk psychology; it *is* psychology.

"A thought comes when it wishes, not when I wish," said Nietzsche. In some form, all people know this, but then again they let this thing they call reason interfere, or else the will. The artist perceives Nietzsche's thesis best of all, and will consciously labor to make his unconscious fruitful. What a fertile garden was Bach's unconscious mind, from which he could gather fruits in every season, and without limit.

It is the creative man's *business* to cultivate this hidden garden with his conscious labors, the labors of creative order; the labor of directing thought into one, and away from, too many directions; the labor of excluding, interfering or distracting notions and personalities (the weeding process—how many an artist has been accused of self-ishness in this taxing job); the labor of selection, once the fruit becomes opulent, of putting to order the agony of riches.

Undoubtedly those who have achieved early mastery have more easily learned the habits of soul-gardening, and think little of it, while those who have arrived late must strive constantly and consciously to achieve it. Somehow, the soil of every man has boundaries, and if (as with Schubert, Mozart, Purcell or Mendelssohn) it is overworked in early years, there is little likelihood of its later recovery; and it becomes idle to speak of what these men of genius "might have achieved" had they survived an early death. Who knows whether it was not a premonition that set their desperate energies to work, or whether the energies destroyed the body and the soul before-times, or whether some unseen Apollo may not have charitably closed the eyes of his earthly favorites, sparing them the fruitlessness of exhausted middle years?

What is behind the feeling of tonality? The pitch sense, certainly, and yet it is widely believed that the pitch of today may be considerably higher than the pitch of Beethoven's day. Vaughan Williams is said to have possessed Beethoven's tuning fork, whose a is far from coinciding with ours of today. No key is more characteristic than c minor, and we find its quintessence preserved from Alessandro Scarlatti through Bach, Mozart, Beethoven, Schubert, Brahms and even Rachmaninoff. Nevertheless, what is c minor to us, may have been Beethoven's c-sharp minor, or else his c minor may physically be our present b minor. From this we may deduce not only that "absolute pitch" is relative, but more importantly, that tonality feelings probably have a stronger basis in the tactile instrumental sense than in pitch itself. C minor has a very unique feel on the keyboard, and the aforementioned composers were primarily keyboard virtuosi. It has also a decided character in the strings and even in the winds.

Similar reasoning could be applied to other tonalities, more particularly perhaps d minor, f major, e-flat major and c major. A rewarding study could be made on the subject of how tonalities retain their character while not retaining their pitch.

The Chinese painters liked to paint remembered scenes. The memory simplified and abstracted. It excluded the superfluous. And yet their taste seldom led them into total abstraction. Something of each side, they must have felt, should remain in the other. This may explain the mystery in much of their art. Design and object were intermingled, and since neither was ever wholly revealed, both seemed limitless. It was a marriage of the tangible with the intangible.

The impulse to abstract is ancient. But in our time we make it a party matter. You are objective or you are abstract, just as you must vote Republican or Democrat. Does this not seem a limitation? Can an artist afford to be so partisan? Or else, politically stated, can he afford not to be partisan? Has he the courage to resist the narrow spirit of coteries?

The analogy with music is not entirely clear. Music seems the most nearly abstract of the arts, by very nature; but perhaps that is because we habitually think of only our five senses, forgetting a kind of sixth sense of interior feeling, the sense of tension and release, muscular movement, the visceral feeling (all connected in a way with the sense of touch, but never quite the same). So we may say that music springs as much from the *sixth sense,* as from that of hearing, but in part too from the sense of touch and of sight, for we are affected not only by musical sounds, but by their analogies of appearance. Who has not at some time translated the forms of trees, of clouds, of hills, inadvertently into melodies? But, being the least palpable, music begins, if not belongs, closest to abstraction.

To learn from the ancient Chinese, the composer should patiently allow his materials of life to digest in his inner self, seek no immediacy for their expression, let its unsung melodies enter into his memory, its discords and resolutions, its pains and pleasures. Later they may be distilled into a music that envelops all in simpler beauty, charity along with anger, comfort with despair, harmony with discord, solace with violence, tenderness with passion, and rain with the sun. This tempering will be found in Shakespeare, in Beethoven and in Rembrandt. *Let him make himself rich in things forgotten.* Or, as Robert Frost put it:

> The present
> Is too much for the senses,
> Too crowding, too confusing,
> Too present to imagine.

As to whether a composer should or should not write at the piano, there is much unnecessary to-do. First it was importantly announced that Bach and Mozart never wrote at the piano, and later it was bruited about with equally well-documented fatuity that Stravinsky wrote everything at the piano. It would take only a glance at the relative harmony in the two instances to show the reason for the difference. Besides, Bach and Mozart were prodigies, masters at an age when Stravinsky just began his writing, and that too makes a difference. The habits formed in infancy are unique and unconscious. Chopin wrote everything at the keyboard, but then his music is keyboard-conceived, and could hardly have been born of the most disciplined mind without the guidance of those searching, auditive fingers of his.

A man may hear his own music well enough without playing, and may still wish to exercise his tactility in conceiving it. On the other hand, he may wish to avoid this very tactility, for fear of falling into improvisational piano patterns, when writing not for the piano. Then, too, modern harmony can seldom be fully heard inwardly at first encounter, and needs the keyboard. The writer may be of that school, however, that believes there is no need to hear the final sound so long as all the voices follow their own "logic," and produce their harmony in drifting haphazard. He may be a randomist.

Corresponding to the harmonic dissonance, one may speak of an *acoustic dissonance.* If the tones of any triad be so grouped as to violate the most nearly normal distribution of overtone sounds, one may create with the same chord at once a harmonic consonance with an acoustical dissonance (normally the overtones come nearer together the higher they are above the root tones). Thus Beethoven, in the opening statement of his Thirty-two Variations (which could well be called his Passacaglia in C Minor), bunches the minor chord in the bass in close position, and poses his trumpet-like theme two octaves above the bass note, creating a dramatically strident and discordant sound without use of a "discord." Beethoven was far too inventive of new uses of chords that it could ever be said that this effect was not intentional, or a mere convenience to the hands. Indeed, his feeling for *distribution of notes* within the chord is so individual, one can often identify him from hearing but a single chord. Was ever a sound so uniquely Beethoven's as the first chord of the last movement of his last sonata?

The whole secret of creation is to begin all over again; and that is to begin with nature, and not on the work of others.

What then is this nature? It is *man in nature;* physiological, sociological, political, musical man; man breathing, talking, singing, walking, dancing, loving, seeing, listening; man in pain, man in ecstasy, man in anger, man in revolt, man in wonder, man in battle, man in perplexity, man in prayer, man in thought, man in repose; man seeing himself in nature's moods and forms.

But music growing out of others' music, that is art at second hand, a building over a building, a bush growing out of a tree, a parasite. But the language must first be learned. The truly unique music of the century came from men with the severest classical training. They learned from early models (best to teach from, impossible to recreate today); then later went to one of nature's many sources. But they are not therefore themselves a source, though they may be emulated as example.

Surely then I must first learn the king's English in music. But the special language of one person, whether it be Hindemith, Joyce, or Picasso, has nothing for me unless my heart tells me it is also my own (that he has formulated and anticipated what is in me too, though unspoken).

*Most of invention in music is a discovery.* This is why Goethe so objected to the term *composer,* which hints at contrivance, manipulation, paraphernalia, artifice, stratagem, fabrication.

The bar-line has come to be so closely associated in the modern mind with the recurrent strong, or "down" beat, that we overlook its office as a point of *orientation*. This is why composers give us irregular bars, along with irregular metres, for it is clear that irregular metres could be, and have been, placed within regular bars. Indeed, the composer (and the conductor as well), should always consider whether he wishes the irregular beat to *coincide* with the irregular stresses of his rhythm, or to *contrast* with them. For example, the rhumba, supposedly of Caribbean origin, has mostly the metre, 3-3-2, which adds up to 8. Thus it can be beat in an uneven 3, as in Example 11; or it can be beat in cut time or alla breve, as in Example 12, in which latter case its accents, with the exception of the first beat, create syncopations. I do not say which is the better of the two, but their effect is manifestly different, and here again we have evidence how important it is *to see music while hearing it*, since the distinction would be wholly lost on a record.

EXAMPLE 11

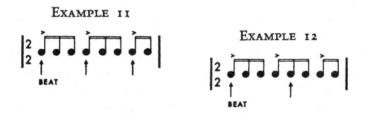

EXAMPLE 12

Most polyphonic music gains by being dressed in regular metres (wherein the bar is only a point of reference), since its manifold voices are bound to have stresses on any and all beats, and seldom coincidentally. I have asked students to place Bach's theme of the fugue in E-flat Minor (Vol. I, Well-Tempered Clavier) in any metre of their choice, and have received widely varying replies. The commonest proposal is a bar of 3/4 with the first tonic note used as an upbeat, a logical choice, but not Bach's.

Total barlessness has little to recommend it, apart from cadenzas. Complete freedom results only in lack of orientation. In point of fact, nearly any piece of bar-less music can be barred easily enough, and usually is, temporarily, for purposes of learning. Liszt's use of the dotted bar, however, has virtue as a compromise between freedom and the convention of regular bars.

Modern music likes to get away from what it feels to be the strait jacket of four-square rhythm. One need only listen to spoken words without music, to see that all poetry is read in a manner impossible to capture in our system of rhythmic notation. The very early Gregorian music probably enjoyed this freedom (later lost, and indeed only partially recovered in the renditions of Solemnes, the more persuasive for their otherwise excellence, but largely recovered in the important researches of Giulio Silva, of San Francisco). Popular and folk singers have always departed freely from the regular beat, whatever its steady accompaniment. The African influence, too, has brought about numerous freedoms, not only in rhythm but in pitch and scale. The modality and metric irregularity of the Anglo-Appalachian folksong have given us other freedoms; in tone production as well as in vocal prosody. All these together give the American musical author a wider range of rhythmic, metric and tonal freedom than is enjoyed by writers abroad.

The color sense shows itself in that a composer will sometimes choose a metric unit for its appearance to the eye. What a fine set of black pages Beethoven managed in his final sonata! Fancy how disappointing if all the thirty-seconds were reduced to eighths. He had the Rembrandt musical sense, as indeed Rembrandt had the Beethoven sense in color. Contrarily, how much better a fine old chorale is when written in half notes instead of, as in so many modern hymnals, in quarter notes. A good score always makes a good picture.

Memory is an asset, but too good a memory may be, for the author, a liability. "With my memory," Toscanini once said, "I could not be a composer." It is not a matter of quantity, for there is hardly a limit to what the memory can contain; but it is very much a matter of preoccupation. New thoughts cannot spring up in a mind loaded with old works, most of all, the masterpieces. Their power is too overwhelming. The creative mind, too, needs memories, but not the memories of great masterpieces, burning the mind with the heat of immediate utterance. This was the tragedy of Mahler, of Anton Rubinstein, and, to a lesser degree of Cherubini, Weber, Mendelssohn, Liszt, Strauss, and Rachmaninoff—all writers who were far too much absorbed with public concerts and institutions to realize themselves to the full as creators of music. The habits of invention and of interpretation are very dissimilar; and each being cumulative, they allow for no frequent or easy interchange.

"Our early revolt against sham civility," said Dreiser, "has resulted in nothing save the abolition of all civility." Could there be any better proof of this than some of our later music? Which art can show more wilful intransigence, more of the *épater le bourgeois* spirit, more disrespect, contumely, and virulence; all displayed as if bad manners were the badge of truth and sincerity, as if to spit in a man's soup were honester than to exchange a decent "good morning." Civility has indeed improved in business and industry, but strangely in the arts it has gone in the opposite direction.

However, one must allow that some modern art, a great deal perhaps, is conceived from *the challenge to make beauty of un-beauty,* to realize the anomaly of extremes, to wed opposites. But even this, when carried on indefinitely, becomes a perversity. What, shall we grant that all beauty today resides only in ugliness? The careless reasoner may presently reverse this idea, too, and say, in ugliness is all beauty. Finally, as in the issue between good and evil, when we boil the difference down to definition, and explain all in social and psychological terms, *there remains little distinction and no morality.* But this represents a total surrender of the heart to the mind, hardly the province of the artist, but very much that of the sophist.

Bloch used to ask, "What has he to say?" What indeed does *saying something* in music mean? It is easily felt, yet not easily defined. We say there is matter, and there is manner. When I am conscious of manner, I usually conclude there is not too much matter. When I am conscious of matter, then I am not surprised if the manner also is good, and the less I am aware of it, the better it probably is. When a man tells me, "I used this technique," or "I did this as an experiment," or "I tried for this effect," or "I feel it this way," I am likely to be more doubtful than convinced. Finally the question must resolve itself into, "What is he?" a question seldom put nowadays by the professionals. They are more apt to ask, "What is he not?" inspired by certain notions about legitimacy, bastardy, and party loyalty.

Whatever a man's powers, unless they are *driven to their limit,* they will never come to their fullest flowering. It takes a war to make a great general, a threatened catastrophe to make a great statesman, a great corruption to make a great reformer. Great occasions are always in the making, both by us and despite us. Great occasions there are for art, too; times when the expectation is high, the level high. But the artist can sometimes himself be the great occasion, or at least foster it. Just waiting for it is like just waiting for "inspiration." The more he prepares himself for it, believes in it, the sooner it will come. The artist and the occasion are mutual.

While an artist mostly works alone, he too requires some community of enterprise. For his work includes also his nonwork, his fertility requires fallowness, *his creation needs comradeship*. He is terrified to be alone, not while at work, but while he is at rest.

In all of art's best periods, creative people were brought together, and thus we had Pericles' Athens, the Medici's Florence, Elizabeth's London, Goethe's (and later Liszt's) Weimar, Beethoven's (and later Brahms') Vienna, Emerson's Concord, Lowell's Boston and Manet's Paris. These were by no means smooth waters, but they were lively.

*Creative talent, if joined, does not add up, it multiplies.* If a single writer, painter or composer is given a residency on some college campus, the intention is benevolent, but it fails to understand that the greater part of the isolated artist's energies must go into overcoming the sheer indifference or ennui of his surroundings, the yawning apathy that envelops him, in a climate of creative unbelief. "A singer needs him a guitar," quoted Frank Warner of a Tennessee mountaineer. Likewise, an author needs another, or more than one other, to supply, if not resonance or harmony, then at least a counterpoint to his own thoughts. "It is good," said Montaigne, "to rub and polish your mind against the minds of others." But there must be those others. A single stone in a brook won't polish in soft mud alone.

The children deserve the attention of our best talent. No age is too early for the cultivation of taste. *Good music is as easy to teach and to learn as poor music.* By poor music I mean not light, or popular, or even modern dance music, but music of indifferent, meretricious, tawdry and untalented kind, such as many of our hymns and teaching pieces, nearly all "piped-in" music, music supposedly good enough for "instructional" entertainment or even "devotional" use, but not good enough to be acceptable as music; watered-down insipid, untalented, insincere, and imitative stuff.

The greatest masters, almost without exception, left melodies simple enough for any child to learn, if one knows where to look for them. The folksongs of the world are innocence unlimited, and what better introduction could children have to the melodic geography not only of their own nation but of other nations, than these records of a peripatetic Orpheus' wide wanderings. And why not a host of new melodies, taxing our living authors with precisely the opposite problem as is posed by the sophisticate world of symphonies and quartets —the problem of simplicity? How relieved a composer should be, to be shed of the responsibility of being always original or profound, or of doing "big" things, most of which fall soon enough of their own weight, or else remain in cold storage.

There is another challenge in the children's world, and that is to find the musical counterpart of what is being done in painting with children, under the enlightened guidance of a great many artists. The advantage in painting is that it requires no literacy. To offset this in music, the tape could take the place of the drawing paper. Nearly all children above the age of four make tunes to words, words to tunes, and stories and dances too, all of which, under the guidance of teachers who understand when to speak and when to be silent, could develop into something very interesting. Not that children should not acquire musical literacy, but the mistake is to believe that without this literacy they cannot make music, an improvisatory child music.

Who knows the labors of simplification that go into the smallest lyric? All the emphasis today is on expansion and development, all the awards to *length* and *size*. The simple is mistaken for the obvious, and so most authors essay a complexity which, if examined closely, could well prove to have been easier to achieve than the simple.

Every writer knows times when a subject appears in a variety of dresses, all pretty much alike, but also slightly different. Between these many, it may be hard to choose. Yet, however equally they attract him, he should school himself to select the fewest possible, in consideration of the performer who, in memorizing the work, need not then be made to suffer undue confusion. *A difference must be enough different to justify any difference at all.*

Much may be achieved through little, or little through much. In America we usually praise the size of the apparatus rather than the achievement. To head a multimillion enterprise is reckoned greater than to write a little song that will go down the ages.

Some men in music are remembered by but little. One opera immortalizes Pergolesi, Purcell, Moussorgsky, Gounod, Flotow, and Bizet. One song is remembered of Boehm, of Rouget de l'Isle, of Henry Clay Work, one verse of Francis Scott Key. The essential music of Chopin, Wolf and Franck could be played in two or three evenings. As in the hydrostatic paradox, the water in a pipe connected with the sea rises as high as the sea itself. *There is no correlation between worth and size.*

# THE
# OBSERVER

\*

# *Of*
## *the Environment*

> *It's a complex fate being an American, and one of*
> *the responsibilities it entails is fighting against a*
> *superstitious valuation of Europe.*
>
> HENRY JAMES

A generation or two ago, the professional world was wider and freer than today, and the academic narrower. Music was not so formal and inaccessible then. A man could take a chance. A failure was a setback, but not necessarily artistic suicide. And there was a regional spirit. The Chicago Symphony served Chicago, where I grew up, and the Middle West, its performers and writers. It enjoyed the same independence as Chicago's university. The city was proud of its arts and vied in all of them with New York and Boston. Music, while it had fewer musicians, used them better, gave them more to do. Every major city was an autonomous reservoir and headquarters for talent. The art had not yet achieved the omniverous centralization of today, rivalling in efficiency the A. T. & T., and secured with policies so vast and political that anyone knocking at its door unarmed with acres of reputation would feel embarrassed to take up such influential and expensive time as reigns within.

The arts need a home in order to be at home. They must be more than just an ornament to everyday life. They need dignity and status. If we are not willing to support them, why then support the schools in which artists are developed? Is the expense too great? Well, perhaps it will prove more expensive not to support them, for nonsupport leads to unemployment, all the ills of frustration, and to those pathetic devices whereby employment is forced upon society where there is no need for it. Nonsupport drives most of our best talent into the educational field, where teaching thrives in useless self-multiplication, and exaggerates thereby the imbalance between supply and demand. For as things are today, *the professional outlets are steadily narrowing while the ranks of the profession are growing.* The bottleneck narrows while the bottle swells.

The arts are not self-supporting and indeed never have been. The public has been given a fictitious picture of the earnings, honors, and rewards enjoyed by artists and musicians, a picture that cannot afford to reveal what goes on backstage. Not that more should be spent on the arts; only that less should be misspent.

Let it not be said of the artist, in Thoreau's words, "You are paid for being something less than a man." *The artists of America have a right to their manliness,* a right to the art's responsibilities as well as to its rewards. They are ready for it, but there is no proof short of actual trial and experience.

The great fault of American patronage is that it tries to legislate, and thereby manipulate, musical progress. Better it were if it helped make conditions favorable to such progress. Right now, the patron is mostly afraid of his own taste and judgment (for which he can hardly be blamed in the present state of confusion), so he gives his money to large philanthropic corporations, and they in turn give out fellowships, prizes, grants, and commissions. To guard their disbursements, they establish *policies,* mostly as invulnerable to misuse as they are imperceptive of real needs (which are always unpredictable, and quite often too modest and personal to fit into such a large and costly frame). As a result, philanthropy becomes as wasteful as is the general "expanding economy" to which it owes its existence. The bigger it becomes, the more does it attract coteries and those who have the time, disposition and political sense to shape their projects to its policies; and the more does it become inaccessible to those others content to stick to their lasts.

"Stick to your last" was good advice to the shoemaker before the time when his apprentice or his inferior discovered it was more profitable to make, or manipulate, or turn to account, the laws of the shoe trade, by which he could put his master out of business.

The conditions favorable to progress are simply those of any learned profession. Music must have a roof over its head, a little support (not too much, either), and some good will. A school answers this need only partially, since it is only a place of training where people pay to learn what they hope later to be paid for.

Right now there are too many musicians in the field (nearly all engaged in the business of making yet more), not because the opportunities are so great, but because they are so small. Were there more *real* places for musicians, there would be more selectivity, since real, and not fictional or contrived standards would operate.

A few dozen regional and independent (I mean independent of New York control, whether by money or management) opera houses and theatres (the stage is no better off than music), with resident artists and orchestras, would be the best immediate answer. All Europe has had these for generations, and has provided them mainly for home talent, in direction as well as performance and authorship. For the first time in history, our government has even been talking about all this. But there is no reason why state and municipal governments should not assume this responsibility, as well as the national government, just as they support education, science, and welfare.

Shall it be said that the richest of nations, which can afford more music education than the world has ever seen, cannot support music itself?

Until this is achieved, however, the only agents that can afford even a token program in the interim, something to prime the pump (let us say a half dozen theatres, or even one or two) are the large foundations. They are also the only agents that can afford the cost of pushing through the expensive legislation needed (in the face of the cultural apathy of most legislators, senators and congressmen). Instead, they lend support to the very orchestras and operas who have resisted a national and regional music. They wash their hands, Pilatically, of the real issue, the while they immerse them in its sacerdotalism.

As for the small patron, how much better it would be if he gave himself the pleasure and honor of helping genius individually, rather than swelling the pockets of the disbursing corporations. He will make mistakes, but on a small scale compared to those of the giants, and probably learn from them, too. Patronage, like anything else, takes practice and experience. To give wisely and well is no mean achievement.

America has built at once from the top down and from the bottom up, and gives little thought to the gap between. With the aid of patronage, operas and symphony orchestras have been gathered abroad and reassembled here in gala splendor. At the same time, schools of music have been built and endowed with a lavishness unknown to history. Virtually all patronage has gone either to youth in the schools, or to the great professional orchestras and operas harboring the accepted stars, mostly from abroad. Little has been done for all that lies between learning and a career, that is, for the man or woman ready and trained for professional life. Money gives us a stalactite and a stalagmite, but will not allow that the two unite.

Europe taught well at first, in the days when our orchestras were founded. It was a bold stroke, to plant symphonies in full professional regalia in the American sticks. But we paid for the instruction, and offered large rewards in honors, emoluments, and hospitalities; besides being very good learners. The instructor should have felt a certain obligation, once the pupil was ready for it, to let him try his own wings; nay, even, in Bronson Alcott's words, "to defend him against his own personal influence." A generation or two might have sufficed, as in medicine and chemistry, but now it is getting on six or seven generations, and we have not cast off the apron-strings. Until we do, we cannot know our powers. Only this; that faith in the effort has a curious way of assuring success in the result, since in art *the expression is a measure of the intention itself.*

It is all a matter of standards, we are told; we will have only "the best," since we can pay for it. Clearly, we would rather buy than build. Every imitation of, and contest with, European contemporary music demonstrates *that we are interested more in impressing the world than expressing ourselves.*

Sooner or later the musician learns that only a New York recital will "get him ahead." And so he sacrifices comfort, money, surroundings, family, security, and beauty of the environment, for the "big chance" in the big city. Somehow he manages to hang on, living by hack work, handouts, patronage or foundational help, and is rewarded, at best, by the excitement of being at the spearhead of the nation's musical life.

"Now come the realities," in Abram Chasins' words. "He must first make a huge investment or throw in the sponge." Mr. Chasins then describes with admirable exactitude (*Speaking of Pianists,* Knopf) the aftermath to all these sacrifices, and concludes with these words: "What I am describing has forced most of America's greatest talents of the last quarter century to abandon all hope that within their lifetimes either their government or their fellow creatures would become sufficiently interested, informed, and indignant to act and improve their lot, . . . within a regime that denies their fundamental rights that belong to all others. . . ."

Others remain or go where they are needed, that is, in the provinces, but instead of being esteemed for this sensible procedure, they become progressively more estranged from the nation's professional vortex; and then discover themselves severed no less from their particular region's main musical rewards, since the region's patrons and authorities act in willing, if unwitting, confederation, with the agents of metropolitan centralization and monopoly.

The eminent musicologist, Dr. Paul Nettl, once compared America with ancient Alexandria, observing that the outstanding characteristic of that era was not that it created culture, but that it preserved and commented on it. Similarly, he stated, in America the cultivation of the music of the past "has a significance which, in my opinion, overshadows the cultivation of native music." This is bravely spoken. It takes more than ordinary courage to tell a parcel of Apollo's nephews to settle down to an embalming career, or to persuade the graduating varsity to go into orders and take vows of celibacy. To a nonhistorian like myself, the comparison between Cleopatra's Alexandria and modern Washington seems oddly incongruous. As well imagine Alexandria sacking Caesar's Rome, as expect the living American Muse to remain in the bleachers. We may not be lions, but would probably hold with Ecclesiastes that a "live dog is better than a dead lion." Nevertheless, Dr. Nettl's thesis does not fall on deaf ears. America has a well-established habit of contrition before musical Europe, quite unlike its other habits. It still acts the role of the familiar music pupil who has been carefully nurtured by his teacher, perhaps not without certain expedient motives, into habits of dependence. His outstanding talent, at least on the surface which Dr. Nettl sees, is obedience, and his most highly praised habit is imitation. A few have challenged the authorities, but they are easily silenced with silence.

Over the arch of the Royal Theatre in Copenhagen are engraved the words, "Not only for amusement."

Why is it that we stand all education on its head and insist on teaching children that all work is play, and then teach adults that all play is work? Children should be taught habits of work, and their elders should be retaught play. The amateur's path to art is enjoyment. There must be plenty of labor to deepen it, but the end is pleasure rather than erudition. We have a lingering Puritanism that insists on souring the divine dish of art in our halls of learning.

The decline in the craft and the standards of piano-building are not a negligible factor in the general decline in piano study (each is of course modified by the other). A generation or two ago, America manufactured a good half dozen different makes of piano, nearly all of the first class. Every major city had its own builder. Assembly-line methods, the kiln drying of wood, the merging of firms, the slow disappearance of skilled craftsmen, the emphasis on ornamental, pocket-sized pianos, the shift to passive musical experience through records and radio, and the sheer pressure of competition through advertisement—all these have contributed to a situation where there remain in the entire world less than a half dozen manufacturers of pianos approximating the first class.

Upright pianos have long gone out of fashion, and consequently at small cost one may now acquire an excellent used instrument, often superior to the "grands" of recent make, and incomparably better than the mini-pianos, with their insufficient sounding boards. In general, the larger the piano, the better its tone, since good basses need long strings. Many a concert grand (usually of nine-foot length) which no longer satisfies professional standards can be acquired at small cost, since few are willing to burden their period-planned parlors with such a commanding, if handsome, object.

Pianos have not the endurance of violins. Nevertheless, a piano of good make may be close to a century old and yet warrant repair and reconstruction in preference to buying any one of a number of new instruments. New actions, new strings, and oversize pins (to prevent slippage in an old pin block, with attendant mistunement), represent only a moderate outlay. The insertion of a new sounding board is a larger operation, entailing shipment to the factory; but even that is often justifiable.

Foreign pianos, particularly the French, generally have easier actions than the American pianos. This facilitates rapidity, but it allows for less range of tone. The best European pianos cost less than ours, duty and shipment included, but there remains some doubt as to whether they survive our temperature extremes (most of all, the dryness of overheated rooms).

"The object of art," said Sherwood Anderson, "is not to make a saleable picture. It is to save yourself. The point of being an artist is that you may live." It takes energy to live well and be happy. You are surrounded by people who subsist on your energy, and give none in return. "I am the ice-cream soda," said Bloch once, "with many straws sucking my juices." *But art, like love, gives energy in receiving it.* You work to impart this zest to others, wishing not only to communicate, but to receive communication. Appreciation is also a communication, likewise understanding, love, and respect. You are respected for your achievement or quality, but you convey your respects to your respectors in making music. Without respecting them, you may perhaps still receive some of their respect, but certainly never quite deserve your own. Great conquerors, like Napoleon, are often adored even though they despised their adorers. But they could never be great artists, holding this view.

"You may see how a man would fight by the way in which he sings," said Carlyle. I believe Beethoven, when he remarked to a friend during the shelling of Vienna, that had he studied military science he would be the man to rout Napoleon. The heroic personality of a Beethoven, if channelled into the strategy of a war to defend liberty could well have given the Corsican pause.

It is not that your long labors must prove themselves in *success* (which is of course worth striving for). But they bear fruit in you as any enlightening, elevating, nonbrutalizing, nonvulgarizing labor will do. Life wholly unorganized could be unendurable just as would disorganized music. The arts offer you a worthy kind of organization, and help you to save yourself. Despising art when it does not also bring success is like despising love when it does not make you a libertine.

It is interesting that in the slow-moving Europe of the seventeenth and eighteenth centuries, there was more community of spirit between the musicians of the various nations than there is in our age of telephones, radios, and jet flights. Only in the modern essays at a deliberate denationalization, such as Schoenberg's system, do national boundaries become vague; and this could hardly be thought a proper comparison, since this music, despite its immense propagandization, has never achieved any degree of mutuality between the writer and his public.

There is some hope in the speculation that the rapid levelling of all the world may also produce new differences; that nature, or language or nativity, will somehow break the common beam of a universal socialization (or industrialization, or intercommunication) into the separate colors of nations, races and regions and dispositions; offering us new compensations for the pathetic loss of distance, isolation and difference.

The first duty of the artist is to resist everything that tends to make him the mass-man. He is mostly considered useless. Well then, let him use this uselessness to good purpose. If we must accept the assembly line to make cars, then it is all the more important to oppose its invasion into our private lives, our recreation and our education.

But he is mostly doing no opposing, and our homes, our schools and our recreations are all being made over into the image of our ant-like industry. Leisure is used now to sell what labor produces in mounting excess and superfluity. We get no respite from Uncle G. E., and we can find no retreat in the wilderness that has not prepared us a grinning welcome from one of Uncle's ubiquitous cousins. Go to the innermost recesses of the Grand Canyon, and you can be certain of advice on what to smoke and what deodorants will render you kissable, scientific confidences on what oil will save your motor from corruption, and intimate notes on what insurance will make dying a positive pleasure.

But if the artist is to assume his ancient and honorable role as exemplar of the free man, he should appropriately begin his reforms in his own profession, than which none is more degraded in servitude to monopoly management, union massmanship, commercial centralization, public vulgarity, and nauseous surfeit.

We made a great to-do when Furtwaengler was proposed for the Chicago Symphony. He had indeed stood up to the Nazis, but he had not stood up 100 per cent, nor had he left Germany, and therefore his presence would have been a menace to American liberty. But his accusers: had they ever so much as cried "boo" to our own musical brown-shirts, from whom the most they had to fear would have been, not midnight arrest and disappearance or recrimination on family and relations, but a little set-back in income or a little dimming reputation? Such vicarious courage is always diverting.

Because some say they "see pictures" during music (Beethoven said he did), many will accuse themselves of lacking imagination, since no such pictures come to them. They should know that there are no prescribed responses to music, no standard reactions, fortunately. *Every man has the right to his own reaction,* including even inattention. (For how often does the performer rise to, and sustain, the level of his music?) "Music," said Lanier, "is love in search of a word." That doesn't call for a Webster or Grove dictionary.

Some music compels, some pleases, and some only disturbs. And if there is music that helps one to forget all music, and to think one's thoughts in the aura of its protection, I would say, that particular music has served a good purpose and the listener is to be congratulated for letting the music stir alive some nonmusical counterpoint of thought.

"We won't mind the piano," says the eager hostess to her pianist guest, who is perhaps quite ready to entertain, provided there is at hand some instrument on which he can produce proper sounds and move his hands with some tactile pleasure, rather than that polished, little semi-piano selected for its Cinderella-like readiness to withdraw into a corner in favor of a shining new television set. He can already picture its rubbery action and its felty imprisoned tones. But he has not the heart to tell his hostess, "But I mind the piano very much; and playing on it offends me, in fact it will spoil my evening, if you insist." And so, if he does not play, he is accounted a refuser, a precious snob, or a man who counts his social pennies, if he shows enough fortitude to beg off.

There remains much of the Puritan in us Americans. We no longer deny freedom of worship, of the vote, of occupation, or even of sex, but man's freedom of communion with nature is ruthlessly prevented at every turn. He is required to accept every *ersatz* for nature, whether in food, in drink, in environment, in smell or in sound. His senses are all assaulted now with substitutes. He is being "sense-washed."

We bulldoze his gardens, his houses, his wildernesses; we fill the air with nauseous sounds; we broadcast industrial odors over entire counties and states; we pollute the air over his cities; we rob him of his natural physical exercise and freedom (and substitute puerile mechanical imitations of these); we herd him into hideous regularities with highways, away from, and not into, nature; we rob him of silences, nature's sounds, and reveries; we meddle everywhere, whether in church, college, school, home or in places of relaxation, with his preoccupations. Yet let him protest and he, like his ancestor suspected of heresy and witchcraft, is charged with subversion—the crime of throwing doubt, not on the church's theology, but the theology of progress, democracy, and the bountiful blessings of an "expanding" waste. He is ridiculed into acquiescence, taxed into conformance, ignored into silence, and his heart is broken if he has not the resistance finally to go "underground."

Well, does this not affect music? We fatuously recount the artistic and human bleakness of Puritan days, and fancy ourselves freer today. Perhaps we have now the Boston Symphony. But I wonder if the services in Symphony Hall hold any more for me than would those in Salem's first church. Beethoven is no more the liberator in Boston today than was Jesus in Salem. He has been cut to size, made correct, sanctified to where only the ordained musical priest may commune with him. *We deify the past so as to degrade the present.* And you'd better not bother any of the deacons with any of your radical notions on this—indeed on anything at all.

Of course there are no banishments, for who today has room for the banished? But the esthetic Polizei do their work quietly and efficiently; they banish into the new and ample dungeon of silence; and who can make himself heard there against the cosmic Brobdignagianity of electro-magnified complacency.

I am often struck with the universal appeal of the most purely regional art; and likewise with the lack of appeal of art that calls itself international or universal. The world clings to the voice of personality in peoples as in men, the more so as it is threatened with the leveling off of industry, organization and communication. Foreign peoples are more interested in American folksong, poetry, drama, jazz, and the Broadway musical, than they are in American experiments in abstractionism, atonality, scholasticism, randomism and dada,

and all researches in artistic Esperanto, or in American orchestras vy-
ing with the European in the rendition of the classics. And yet officially, we do everything to display ourselves in these internationally
competitive fields, rather than put forth what is native and unique.

An artist should be seen as well as heard. A record may reinforce
our impressions of him, but it will never establish him as a personality.
A record does less for the musician than did the silent pictures for
the actor. Not to be seen is an even greater handicap than not to be
heard. If the actor must overact or remake his gesture to compensate
for the absence of speech, so must the musician remake his performance to compensate for being not seen.

But the musical remake reduces, rather than expands his declamatory powers. Accuracy becomes his main concern. He must level off
his extremes, and if he does not, they will be levelled off for him by
the "dial maestro" anyway, all at the cost of a spontaneity impossible
(or else rehearsed—a self-defeating thing) before that grim little
gusto-graph, the microphone, that remorseless stenographer, who records sounds without the smile or frown of the occasion.

With technique at so high a level as it is today, the difference in
performance between one recorded artist and another becomes ever
less perceptible, the more so because all strive for that final orthodoxy,
which the records themselves have evolved as an ideal composite between those few of highest reputation.

There will never be a substitute for a concert. When I am told
that the record relieves a music lover of the need to dress, to sit in a
hall, to rub shoulders with others, to pay admission, and to applaud,
then I know his position toward the art. *Small effort, small reward.*
How could the art survive under such a snobbery?

As for me, I confess that I need to look at a man to know what he
is. I am not musician enough to judge through the ears alone. Once I
have seen him, I will be more ready to hear him without seeing, if
necessary; but then only if necessary. "If you once understand an
author's character," said Longfellow, "the comprehension of his
writings becomes easy." Yes, character.

Art is unique in that it is meant to endure, to outlive the artist
and his time, to outlive many generations. But now we have a new
art that scorns permanence, looks on it as a conceit, an unreality in

the face of so much change and such a universal danger, and takes pride no less in its evanescence than in its up-to-the-minuteness. Not just a popular art, but an art of ultrasophistication. It *makes a virtue of impermanence.*

The Tyrolese peasant of today as always before, when he builds a house, builds it for his great-grandchildren as well as for himself. And while it is seldom new in design, it is, in a way, a work of art. The builder in California takes care that the house he puts up, something that is neither conventional nor art, will need replacing in a generation, thereby assuring the same profitable waste for the next generation of builders. He knows that a well-built house will be the tax-man's first target, the first to fall. And who is safe against the bulldozer, that harbinger of the next tornado of speed and progress? Is it not noteworthy that as our resources dwindle, we squander them ever more wantonly; the wastefulness of the impecunious. Note by comparison, the solidly built houses, farms, stone fences and barns of old New England and the South, built at a time when none could see the end of resources and pioneering. Note Brigham Young's instructions to the Mormon settlers of Deseret, to build houses *so they will last.*

And how is it with the arts? Are not their tax-men busy pulling down the staunchest works of a previous era first of all? With what zeal they already dismember Whistler, Sargent, Eakins, Homer, Cassatt, Bellows, Luks, Sloan, Henri, MacDowell, Griffes, Loeffler, Gilbert, Dreiser, Anderson, Hergesheimer, Bierce, and London. *Can they expect respect, when they show none themselves?* There is a provincialism in time as in place, that sees only as far as the narrow borders of current time and fashion, and puts all else to ridicule. If the fashion is Freud, then all who have not benefited by seeing life through that sad man's eyes are to be pitied. If it is Marx, or Joyce, or Proust, or Schoenberg or Picasso, it is the same. Not that these men gave themselves those protective and advertisive labels by which our textbooks immortalize them, but they were quickly and easily labelled, classified and filed, and the public needs labels to cling to, something to shield it from the unpredictable and inclement weather of thought.

There is no greater myth in our day than communication. *While it binds it also severs.* In it is the same enigma as in transportation, whereby the automobile, claiming to bring nature nearer to the city dweller, succeeds only in removing nature in proportion to her accessibility. Men, too, have become remote in ratio to the immediacy of communication. As the mails, the telephone, and the jet plane conquer distance, so a man builds barriers around himself, and cultivates aloofness. Men will sooner assault an enemy stronghold than run the gauntlet of a few secretaries. The dissocial Beethoven was easier reached than Toscanini, of recent honored memory.

Now that television, radio, and records must fill out time and franchise, the public will think no reputable writer or performer need remain severed from his public. Instead, these new media of communication have created a new aloofness, have established a code of "saleability" and of what is Hearstly conceived as public taste; and they retire before enterprise and ideas into their stronghold of arrogant conformity, repetition, and vulgarity.

It isn't that an artist must be regional or American as a matter of policy (as if he were of some plan or party). He should be regional or native in that which he knows in his bowels and his blood. It has nothing to do with geography or nationalism, save that one expects a man to be most at home where he has lived; and living is more than livelihood or citizenship or birth. James and Whistler belonged as much to an English environment as Mark Twain and Winslow Homer to an American. Thayer's world was Beethoven. El Greco's world became Spain, as indeed to some extent it became the world of Irving, Borrow, and Hemingway. *An artist's nation is his heart.* If he is properly rooted where his heart is, he will be universally accepted as a citizen. But if he thinks he can root himself anywhere or everywhere, he is mistaken. "Menschen, seid umschlungen!" is a universal benediction, coming from a Weimar poet and a Vienna composer. But were it conceived in literary and musical Esperanto, who would heed it?

Men think that a surrounding of beauty will yield a better art. ("Doesn't that view of the ocean inspire you to write?" "You should create a symphony about those sequoias.") Instead, it is a lack of the beautiful or a memory of lost beauty that yields the best art. Men often make what they cannot otherwise have. They produce out of hunger, rather than satiety. The canyons of Manhattan (desolate not alone for their barren stone or their sunless depth, but for their remorseless regularity as well) have sometimes evoked better melodies than the sunny gardens of California.

And yet there is something wrong, if timely, about this too. Art should be not only compensation. Shall nature be denied the song born of itself and be given only that of its devastation? Perhaps the art spirit is offended by the taint of vulgarity that has settled over all open beauty today, presaging vast new rapings and profligations in the name of "better living" and "safer driving."

We have not lived in ancient Greece, or in Florence, or in Goethe's Weimar, but we know those places had a beauty one could depend on, get to know closely, learn to love without fear, without the fear not of war alone (which has always existed), but of a defenseless invasion by the pitiless bully-boys of an omniverous "progress."

An American city running its own music (let us even say, to the extent that it runs its own schools, its sewer system, its parks and politics) would be an interesting place. Favoring its own musicians—not therefore excluding those attracted from elsewhere for good purpose; not dancing to the fiddle of some far off impresario, union Mussolini, syndicate critical sage, or boss of the air, but standing confidently and expectantly on its own; opening its doors generously to its own bright talents, inviting from them the pride, loyalty and dedication warranted by the expectation; supporting chorus, theatre, opera, symphony, letters, painting, sculpture, architecture, solo performance, and all the lesser arts surrounding the greater, and asking in return entertainment, instruction, imagination, beauty—it would within a generation surpass every city of the world, become a modern Florence.

Its glory would reaffirm, yes, advertise, the nation's great foundational principles as no orator's or diplomat's words ever could. For the liberty on which our nation was built, is not an end in itself. It is but a beginning, an emancipation from political tyranny, and once achieved, what then? It offers a clean slate to write on, but *then comes the writing.* "I must study politics and war," said John Adams while laboring on the Declaration of Independence, "that my sons may have liberty to study mathematics and philosophy, in order to give their children a right to study painting, poetry and music."

Liberty yes, but liberty to live where my leisure is not circumscribed by what is profitable to industry, freedom to bring my art in fair competition into the public market, freedom of access to uncombed nature, to simple silence, freedom to labor at what I consider useful.

# Commonplaces

*'Tis the good reader that makes the good book.*
R. W. EMERSON

## PERFORMANCE

Piano playing must indeed be *playing*. The labor consists in preserving the play.

*A good technique obliterates itself.* It gives the appearance of ease in the performance of that which is difficult, of elegance in the portrayal of the inelegant, and of naturalness, however bizarre its assignment.

The piano need bow to no singer. In emulating song it may surpass song itself, just as Prometheus surpassed the gods in striving for godhood.

Without the body there is no spirit. *The highest reaches of art have the lowest foundations.*

The piano's melodic art is an art of *suggestion* rather than of *realization*. Thus it is that the piano as a melody instrument is at once the easiest and the most difficult to master; easiest because its tone is ready to hand, most difficult because this tone must be made to sound as though it were created, in order to come alive.

For a technical judgment of your playing, consult your fellow artist. For a judgment of your art, consult the layman, or else the artist possessed of a stature beyond envy. Only the very innocent or the very wise will give you a truth above party, creed, or coterie.

Some play as if the easy were difficult and the difficult easy. They juggle with bravura and pant with simple melody.

The way you hold the interest in your hearers reveals how you hold it within yourself. In the dull performer, I recognize the dull self-listener.

The realest playing is often pure illusion. This is shown by the player who, when contending with a defective or untuned instrument, succeeds nevertheless in imagining ideal sounds, and transporting his hearers out of all awareness of the piano's blemishes. He compels them to hear *imaginarily* along with himself. This beautiful art is, of course, lost in the recording.

The way a man puts his hand on the piano affects a musician as a brushstroke would affect a painter. The first gesture, like the first sound, reveals the player's sensibility. One knows the artist the moment he begins.

The deviations from a steady tempo which have their origin not in a musical necessity, but in a technical one (such as the crossing of strings, or the changing of pedal, or extended leaps, etc.) are best understood when *seen* as well as *heard*. The listener (and watcher), adjusting to the player's adjustment, the two cancel each other out, and the effect is one of rightness.

The superior artist is not always he with the largest capacity; he is usually one who has *realized* what has been given him to the fullest. The public senses this, and favors fulfillment over dimension.

There is a world of difference between playing correctly and playing arrestingly. The one has the features of life, the other has life itself.

Singing is speech made musical, while dancing is the body made poetic.

The discerning artist will find something of all music in every piece of music.

The *routinier* is convinced he knows himself. He is the perfectionist who believes in his perfection. Parodying Francis Bacon, there is no blemish that hath not in it some perfection; even this perfection.

As to reputation and living, be assured (and consoled) that better men than you have fared worse.

As between innocent arrogance and arrogant simplicity there is little to choose; the arrogant had best be removed.

Of musical learning, it could be said, as of money wealth; the more there is of it, the less it should be seen.

There are today so many good musicians that it is becoming increasingly hard to find a great artist.

The future will want to be treated by us of its past with the same lenity we have enjoyed from those in our own past. It will resist being fenced-in too closely with rules and admonitions. It will sense and savor what we leave in its own way; and we should be glad of that, since it is the natural course of things.

Wherever there is excessive praise, you can be sure that the recognition of new talent and accomplishment is weak.

Any success, untempered with some failure, has little chance of lasting.

There is in the arts scarcely a single great name that did not at some point bribe its way through some dubious political tollgate. Only the failure can afford an unspotted morality. Yet when he meets success in person, he is made to feel ashamed of his very virtue.

If you, as an interpreter, do not serve your own personality first of all, you will not do justice to the personality of the author. *Make yourself his slave, and you make him a tyrant.* The proper bond between author and actor is understanding.

Just as art without animality is spiritless, so is animality without art gross.

Energy is needed for restraint as well as for effort. Restraint indeed is only energy in reverse.

The word "creativity" should be put to rest. There is more creativity often in a performance than in the composition of a work, just as a child may be raised better sometimes by his teacher than by his parents.

The one single trait essential above all others to a first-class artist would seem to be, not accuracy, not brilliance, not dexterity, not memory, not sense of pitch, not even beauty of tone, but *intensity* (whether this shows itself in power, in delicacy, in precision, in color, in timing, in energy, in balance, or in tone).

## STUDY

Whatever is worth learning, is worth exaggerating until learned.

Effort, particularly physical effort, can lead to gluttony, whereby the mind's digestion is unsettled. *Effort must be sufficient to pass beyond itself into ease.*

The piece has not been written that will not wear out its welcome with too much repetition. How quickly we say a certain music is "dated," when it is you or I who may have become dated.

The hands become wooden from disuse or from overuse. The trainer being also the horse, a proper routine of exercise is not easy to establish. How simple to conduct an orchestra, by comparison, and to control the music when you do not have to do the playing too. To lead and follow, both, takes some doing.

Not the least part of gaining facility is removing resistance. We are full of habits of friction and sluggishness and memories of non-accomplishment. The hand, like some child apart from ourselves, can often do more than we know, if permitted. The self must be gotten out of the way in the art's athletics, no less than in its devotions.

As in climbing high mountains, the progress one makes toward the final summits of mastery are often so slow as to be imperceptible. The difference between being there and being *almost there* is something only the Alpinist fully understands.

No one will ever quite learn how much he may *spend* himself and how much he must *spare* himself. Spend too much, and risk exhaustion. Spare too much, and risk missing the best fruits that only a final effort will reveal.

The less convincing a passage is, the more it demands your conviction. A weakness made evident reflects only on the performer. If a work seems to you "weak," eschew it, to avoid the charge either of failure in judgment, or unconviction in performance.

Inspiration has had many definitions. Among them could be that state of mind in which one is willing to hunt down to the dregs for that which will best of all say what is to be said. It is the energy to be patient, with the patience to remain energetic.

Technique is the ability to do what is required. Since music involves every manner of color and proportion, the evocation of moods, the quality of song, along with manual dexterity, technique comes to have a wide meaning.

No task is too great provided you find its appropriate tempo.

The correction of an error should begin at its very heart, and then be framed in ever-widening circles.

The hand teaches the body, the ear teaches the hand, the heart teaches the ear.

While it takes energy to be daring, it also takes some daring to summon up energy: the blood and the will.

The player is always pleasantly surprised at what has happened to a piece after being left fallow for a considerable period. Old stumbling blocks have been smoothed; the difficult is suddenly easy. It is as if busy dwarfs had been at work in the underground of the subconscious. Indeed, without their labor and approval, no work can be said to be fully learned.

The "purist" has the easier course. Believing there is but one way to do a thing, he does not suffer the agonies of indecision between multiple possibilities. "Purism" is virtue without goodness.

Nothing is learned until it is easier to do it right than otherwise. This pertains not only to physical actions, but to the very evocation of feeling.

Have a good and sufficient reason, if you must put aside an art once deeply ingrained in yourself. Otherwise the art will atrophy in you, like an overdeveloped heart in an athlete, after he succumbs to a life of physical ease. Music is a jealous mistress, but is worldly enough to recognize a worthy rival.


## TEACHING

Facility and memorization are what impress the untutored the most, and the initiates the least. Every horse can run, and we think nothing of it. The champion horse runs but a fraction faster than other running horses; but in that small fraction lies a world of distinction.

Time is to the musician what space is to the painter. To see a musical work *in perspective* requires elapsed time, just as to see a picture properly requires distance.

The greatest theorists of history were the masters themselves. They were far too busy with their own discoveries and inventions to lay down any special laws. Besides, they favored the art over its theoretical reportage. Instead of imposing their laws, they lived them.

Those who would argue the validity of a trend reason that the future is to the present as the present is to the past. They argue that the curve of a tendency must continue. They take no account of reverses, exhaustions, and indeed the crooked course of history.

Names, such as "Baroque," "Romantic," "Classic," "School of," "influence": all these are but cages for the birds of song. They domesticate the singer, but have never been known to improve his song, nor make us any happier to hear it.

Our government, instead of paying farmers for not raising hogs, would do better to pay composers for not writing too much music. Not to burden the taxpayer further, it could tax radio for playing far too much music.

Why shall we not say "great," and speak of "genius"? We know what is meant, though we fail in definition. The tribute we deny our living Olympians, we lavish then on plastic and synthetic gods, rich in things, not to emulate, but only to envy. It takes courage today to salute greatness.

There are some who play as if their fingers had traction, and others who play as if their fingers were just bouncing or sliding over the keyboard. Those with traction seem to be headed somewhere, the others are just running for the running itself. It is the same distinction as between those who sing, and those who merely make pleasant sounds, the "vocalists."

Easy it is to demonstrate a detail, a phrase, a passage, a gesture of eloquence. But to incorporate this little polished gem into the whole is quite something else. The sprinter's stride is not that of the marathon runner. The water in my cup is no longer the water in the stream.

Much eloquence begins in pose and affectation. Mannerisms in a young man can spell promise; in a mature man they spell only arrested development.

There is a certain miasma of mediocrity in the midst of which the strongest will succumb to cynicism.

As for our temples of music, let the enterprise win its home, not the home its enterprise. There is no greater reproach than an idle forum.

The Snob, too, has his place, at least on a level with the leveller. It is no worse to affect superiority than to impose mediocrity.

"A ploughman on his legs," said Franklin, "is higher than a gentleman on his knees." Well, in this age of statistics, of polls and majorities resolute only in maintaining their "expanding" prosperity, one man with a mind stands higher than a million surrenderers.

Paraphrasing Pascal, when a student complains of the hardship of his labors, set him to do nothing at all. He may soon find the vacuum of labor and thought harder to endure than the effort of accomplishment.

That a man places the intuitional above the intellectual, does not stamp him as intellectually inferior. Not the least of the intellect's function is to know its limitations. If I am hired as a butler, I am a better butler if I accept my station than if I presume above it. *I become freer when not contending for an unreal freedom.*

Musicology has become the old maid of music, who lectures on the art's courtship, love, marriage, obstetrics, and infant care—all with doctoral, professorial inexperience and aplomb—and yet somehow, through some antiseptic alchemy, manages to reproduce her kind at a disturbing rate.

Most of the art's admonitions come from either those who have given up trying for success, or else from those who have forgotten failure.

## Authorship

The truest originality is not a product of the brain alone. It comes to those who have permitted the digestion of the brain by the heart.

The baggage car learns of speed by following the locomotive. But that does not teach him how to pull.

When you have nothing to say, you can always become complicated.

Whoever takes the view that everything is permissible in art, condemns himself to accomplishing nothing. Without limitation, direction or objective, there is also no compulsion or incentive. You broaden yourself only to discover where you can best be narrow. You limit yourself to move ahead, in doing which you cover ground to a purpose.

It was Toscanini, I am told, who, after a monumental reading of the Beethoven *Ninth*, remarked, while surrounded with adulators, that a performance such as his was not to be measured with the creation of but one good song. Since his departure, I have heard no similar tales of Jovian deference.

It is only when music is personal that it becomes regional; only when regional, national; only when national, international. An international music *per se* has the artistic attraction of Esperanto.

The better your art, the more does it reveal the worst in you, as well as the best. It finally becomes you. Yet the more it tells of you, the more also is there to tell. *You make your art, while it makes you.*

There is no true prediction save uncertainty. And yet he who goes out armed with the vulnerability of the uncertain is the most certain to find something worth finding. Art is full of modern Columbuses who propose to venture forth to discover New York City.

All words about music are, to the consecrated writer, a kind of betrayal, whereby confidences are squandered to the careless, and secrets revealed to the sacrilegious. In the end, a man in music, as one in love, either lives it or talks about it; seldom both.

You do not "polish" a work, over and over again, just to smooth it off. In "polishing," you not only study if you have said things most clearly and truthfully, but *you hunt for new things to say,* new truths. A thought, like a potato, is as good for its sprouts as for its nourishment.

How hard it is to start, as Schumann once said; and then, once the momentum is there, how hard again it is to stop.

"All art is but imitation of nature," has been said often. But what that nature is, that is your vigilant study, and none will finally tell you, in following an art that defies all definition.

Parentage in life is honorable. Why should it not be in art? Each generation must find its own way, but that is no reason for a boastful insultingness toward all that went before.

The inferior artist is content to start where others have left off. He believes that time and progress have given him a higher vantage point from which to go on. The superior man goes forever back to beginnings. He knows that, while the tree has grown, its roots too have changed. He tries to recover the child in himself.

Artists of today are worried to be called "programmatic" or "representational," as if the avoidance of these traits brought about some new reality, as if the subconscious could be portrayed by going subterranean, as if indeed his subconscious were so unique as to be worth revealing.

*The more ancient the roots of art, the better its flower.* The genuine modernists are such by right of a classical background, their credentials were respectable. Unearned background is like unearned wealth. Art is full of pensioners, coupon-clippers, and persons who live by the mails and the ticker tape of "style."

Paraphrasing Descartes, on certain composers of the day: "I scream, therefore I am!"

A man may be driven into genius. It may be his last resort, with his back against the wall.

There is always something mysterious in the discovery that the more you dredge yourself of ideas, the more there remain to be dredged.

Who knows his own thoughts until he begins to write them down?

All striving is toward completion, which, once achieved, conducts the spirit as through the splendid gate of a movie prop suddenly into some sordid backyard again.

We learn only through error. But to do so, we must have the stuff to recognize it. That is why it is said of good artists, they are never fully satisfied. Their self-criticism is always ahead of their accomplishment.

"To think," as Clarence Darrow said, "is to disagree." Likewise to create is to change. Even just to discover is to change, for (as with the photographer) it limits, focuses, frames, compresses, illuminates, and thus alters all relationships. There is a bond in disagreement, and a unity in change, in that it is the unlike that attracts.

No composer is ever up to his music. The pleasure we have in meeting him is not his impressiveness, but the discovery that he is not impressive at all, but likable perhaps.

The artist lives between his wars or in them. He knows little of the peace, of which he is the most passionate advocate.

There is a peculiar stamp of conformance about the modern "original." Men act and do original things, but are not original. They think music is a source instead of a result. They fail to look behind music. They would create flowers out of flowers instead of from seeds.

Harking back to Schumann, Smetana, Hugo Wolf, and Mac-Dowell; they labored up to their insanity to write sanely. Today, the sanest strive to be accounted insane.

An artist cultivates his thoughts by "getting black on white," in de Maupassant's words. The smallest sketch is enough. The harvest of symphonies, books, and paintings begins with the planting of themes, glimpses, fragments, relations, colors, possibilities, fitnesses, in the artist's mind and habit. The littlest may imply the greatest. The uninformed think that art is a continuous harvest, rather than ninety per cent cultivation.

Philosophy and art are ever at odds. And yet neither is complete without the other. An unbeautiful reason is as unsatisfactory as an unreasoned beauty.

Not what I can include, but what I can get along without.

Piazzoni, the painter, once told of an acquaintance just returned from Catalina Island. "Nothing to paint there but Sugarloaf Rock." How, I wonder, does Sugarloaf Rock differ from the Serial Row in drawing all eyes away from the Island's other limitless aspects?

What is uglier than beauty said unmeant? And so the young cannot forgive the old for having made a routine of beauty, and they revolt against it. But they forget that not all old fiddles are mistuned, and that they may contain countless new melodies.

Just as the truth of fact makes the scientist, so does the truth of sentiment make the poet.

Now you must dress your thoughts in ten thousand words, your melodies in ten thousand notes, to be credited.

Genius is simply talent that has effaced itself in its own consummation.

It is not the mountain, the canyon, the ocean, or the sunset that make the inspiration. They simply unlock it, by lifting us out of the clockwork of everyday life.

In San Francisco's Golden Gate Park is a waterfall that starts from the top of a hill. Few question how a stream may gather without a watershed above, just as they do not question how some music can occur without a watershed of experience, tradition, and humanity. They overlook the pipe and the pump.

Talent needs more than a livelihood. It needs a life.

This may be a period of decadence, but does that require that I should celebrate it?

One cultivates temperance in expression, not to temper the message, but to strengthen it. One discovers that others will listen better if the voice is lowered. In tempering, one takes better aim.

An artist must have the wilderness, if only to reconcile him with civilization.

It is a rare bird whose song will not take on a note of bitterness, when singing only in paradise.

The proper acknowledgment by an artist, whether of assistance, or appreciation, or praise or patronage, is a new work. Artists, like our children, thank us through their own offspring.

What is warmth in a music that is all warm? What is dissonance in a bed of discord? What is light without shadow? A work, to be organic (at least a large work) must have nature's contrasts and reliefs; it must have cool as well as warm colors; it cannot live in one long extremity.

One discovery leads to another, and presently a fertile mind is so overwhelmed with ideas that, in order to manage what he already has, he must close the door to more. At this moment he learns the lesson of economy, and realizes that the frugality of the masters springs not from paucity, but from plenitude.

Who listens today? What is there to hear? Those who would listen the most, fear the most to listen. They fear the enemy, the sound that destroys, the invader of song and silence; the intruder who would buy all beauty with his ugliness, thinking to outdistance the means for the end, to recover what he has laid low in his headlong race to return to pre-corrupted nature.

## CRITICISM

Some tastes are narrow; some so broad and watered-down, there is no taste at all. "I know what I like" (the provincial's standard self-gratulation)—is it any worse than "I no longer have dislikes" (the sophisticate's creed of caution)? So open to all, it is harbor to none; so catholic, it has no religion. It says, in effect, "I'd rather never be sure, than ever be wrong."

In the scales of today a theory will outweigh any song.

In business, a man competes with others. In art he competes only with himself. The true function of criticism is to discover to the artist and to the public the outcome of the latter, not the former, contest.

There is a difference between *admiring* an artist and *loving* him. I can admire the ingenuity, the economy, and the invention of Debussy, but I cannot love him like Schubert, the first phrase of whose music draws me into his embrace.

The more science, the less art. The more we study the motivation and working of genius, the harder it is to produce it. We explain the reason and explain away the impulse.

There is the critic who is an artist; and there is the artist who is critic. Things are at their best when there is something of each in the other.

Praise and blame are the artist's climate. It is indifference alone which freezes.

Whenever I hear a man called "perfectionist," I conclude he must be that, and nothing more.

Great new music is as possible in our time as it is improbable. I do not hold with those who overrate the past, any more than I hold with those who, in defiance of the nonbelievers in the present, presume to balance Bach with Gershwin and Beethoven with Stravinsky. I am not a party man in time, any more than in style and nationality. I go to hear a new work in a passive state, and make myself as much as possible an empty slate on which the music may write as it will.

Of more than one who has passed authoritative judgment on the arts, could be said, he:

> Sampled all, rejected nothing,
> Loved little, hated less,
> Talked learned, seldom listened,
> Knew all, felt nothing.

It takes more time than is allowed a critic to be as brief as he must be.

Decadence, like age, is more fact than fault, and its expression may have the virtue of timeliness. It shows in that sentimentality replaces sentiment, subjectivity supplants objectivity, theory outstrips performance, and masculinity and femininity become indistinguishable.

All the arts are today borrowing from each other. An age essentially statistical is more interested in analogy and similarity than in uniqueness and difference.

Newness can be attractive, clean, and healthy, but it is a poor home for the soul of art. It takes some using and weathering to domesticate what is new into harmony with old surroundings.

As to decadent art, there comes a time when truth is easier seen in the mud than in a sky dulled with excessive star-gazing and celestiality.

Not all great art is born of youth and passion. Age and experience have also a right to speak and to be served. No music bears this out more than Beethoven's late works. Here wisdom and compassion have supplanted violence and romance.

The difference between science and art: science rests on proof, art on instinct. And yet science often begins in art, while art often ends in science.

The only tradition that stays alive is that which adjusts to time and place. The graceful yield of tradition to new tastes will assure most nearly that the new tastes respect tradition. Here, as in all else, must be mutuality.

## IN GENERAL

Labor and luck both have a part in success. But the unlucky mostly overrate luck, while the lucky disremember it. Behind all is a mocking spirit through which fame becomes as unsatisfactory to the famous as obscurity is to the obscure.

The conflicts of art are mostly between truth and formality.

All great artists burn the candle at both ends.

The *routinier* in any walk of life looks always forward to a vacation from his labors. The artist's vacations are his moments of complete immersion in work, and all so-called "vacations" are nothing more to him than a recharging of energy to resume his passionate labors.

Like those hunters who express their love for the deer with a bullet, we now express our love of great music by bringing it low with learning. It is something to boast of, to bag a Beethoven.

"Don't rock the boat" is the watchword in these dangerous times. We are not to rock the boat while we mutely watch it heading for the rocks.

An art of democracy is not a democratic art. Only the aristocrat can recognize superiority in the average, and knows the average in the superior. The world's great commoners were the most uncommon of men. And so it is with the artists of democracy (Franklin, Jefferson, Emerson, Lincoln, Whitman).

The one comforting thought of progress: that our sons will see young beauty where for the fathers it has died from wasteful overuse.

The world admonishes you: play the game and forget the fouls. But we have never agreed to the rules.

American society, which runs on the principle of waste, cannot afford the luxury of not enlisting those artists it has so thoughtlessly displaced into the ranks of unessential labor. It cannot afford to abandon them to what would soon develop into the most subversive of all doctrines, namely, economy.

When the editor, the conductor, the scholar, and sometimes the contest judge, read the new score, they read not *its writing*, but rather its *reputation*. They become expert not in scores but in scrapbooks. A whole profession has grown up, whose office is nonreading and cushioned rejection.

Art should be of its time, we say; and yet in the next breath say, "Art should be timeless." It may be possible to reconcile the two, but must we? Good art is of its time at all times.

The machine promised us respite from blood, sweat, and tears. Instead, it has given us noise, speed, and a despair that dries the very source of tears. This may account for some of our recent music.

"The misfortune," said Leonardo, "is when theory outstrips performance." It is the anomaly of the cart before the horse, the servant before the master, the clerk before the creator, the means before the end, the method before the matter, the tool before the craftsman, the gallery before the picture, the temple before the worship, the hall before the music, the philosophy before the sage, the money before the need. It is an ancient blindness, cured and restored in every age.

Science has fairly well ruined art, just as sex has ruined love. Satiated with romanticism, which had the ideal of a self-generating love and art, we turned to the other extreme. Is it better? Art can be sexless but not loveless, and love is unscientific but not artless. As with alcohol, we abolished the saloon with Prohibition, and then put in its place the cocktail bar.

Great music is not a decoration. It makes the frivolous wearer of it uncomfortable. It reproaches our day, whether by its sadness or happiness, making us feel how weak we are in the expression of both.

What greater curse does music suffer, than "Music"?

We resemble the Europeans in that, while we have adopted those of their traits least appropriate and native to ourselves, they have adopted also those of our traits most inappropriate to themselves. We took in their madness in the Arts, and they took in our "better living." Fair trade in poor currency.

How bravely now we exalt the braveries of the past. We revel in Socrates, in Galileo, in Washington, in Beethoven, Rembrandt, Goya, Moussorgsky, Swift, Thomas More, Whitman, Van Gogh. (It takes the same courage to choose a path into neglect, unpopularity, poverty, obscurity, posthumity as it does to defy tyranny and oppression.) *We love them for what we dare not be.* We exalt courage in proportion as we do not exercise it. These brave men are safely in the past.

Someone said of the Germans that they came to know more and more about less and less. An American replied that his countrymen preferred to know more and more about more and more. That is commendable, said a Frenchman, but it overstrains the proposition. It seems to me, said an Englishman, that the real trend of the times is to know less and less about more and more, and it's universal.

Some present music forces the listener into a state of reluctant reasoning, by default of all else. It is often praised as "interesting."

There is no greatness that can survive the assault of modern statistics; they are the final leveller.

Art has no worse enemy than "security." In the past, the higher the aim the greater the risk. Now artists talk of guarantees, rights, and insurances, as if they were laboring on some production line, against whose deadly monotony and threat of a shut-down they needed the state's protection. In revenge, society grants them their security (in this most insecure of days), but nothing more.

"But you don't understand," said the master-minder of the tandem management monopoly that has been running the nation's music for a generation, "we're in business." Plainly the assumption was that I as a musician am not. "We go strictly by the box office." "Will you show me the box office then," I said, "that controls medicine, education, the courts, the armed services, public works, the forest service, the parks, reclamation—shall I continue?" I can think of no learned profession where the agent has the presumption to demote the expert into the role of amateur. "Indeed," I should add, "by what right do you pocket the fees I have earned?"

In the art codes of today, novelty is made to look like daring. Daring may be courage, it may even be morality; yet it is often only ostentation. But novelty needs no daring when it has become the fashion, is seldom more than ingenuity, and sometimes it is only an unrecognized copy of another's ingenuity. As things are, it now takes courage not to be novel, and honesty of motive has become the "pearl of great price."

In early days, the American surpassed his America. Today America surpasses the American. Pioneering has become land wastage and real-estating. Liberty has become trespass. Independence has become neighborly disregard. The hunger for the arts has become satiety. Learning has become scholasticism. The sweet yearning of music has become the sour wail of an esthetic distemper.

A little doing is worth a library of learning, in getting at the heart of an art. And so in the arts' wisdom, the amateur can often surpass the scholar. Just as love is understood only by love, so art is revealed only in its own exercise.

The spectator follows the play in a game of baseball. But the player *feels* the play, as well. For him it is more than a game; it is bones and muscles, bruises and triumphs. It is the difference between witnessing and being.

Some decadence there is in every period. Indeed, what could furnish a better background for new affirmation than a prevalent denial?

How well do Americans deserve America? They reward its gifts with wanton greed. Instead of accepting, they plunder. It is the artist's duty to defend his America, first of all from its own thieves.

Music has of late been made a political tool. All these international interchanges of orchestras and artists are meant to prove something; quite what it is, we wonder, since most of what we send abroad comes from there to begin with. It is America posing as a competitor in energy, efficiency, and expenditure.

Patronage (whether private or foundational) undoes its very purpose the moment it insulates itself in hard policies. The best talent is by nature exceptional, and there is no policy founded on exceptions. Policy puts to sleep the exercise of judgment.

A good man respects his past as well as his future, is as considerate to parents as to children. America is too ready to obliterate its past (all but the political), while Europe is too unwilling to live it down.

Why must we always fight our government to save what it should be the first to protect? Who legislates for beauty, learning, and art, and all that these require as well as give?

Once it was Alaric the Goth who captured Rome. Now it is the captain from Madison Avenue who wields, instead of a sword, a cosmetic smile, which gives one to wonder whether he should or should not believe in his baritonal "sincerity." He is like one of whom was said long ago, "Thou singest like a bird called swine."

What good were art in a world of art; a lamp lit in the sunshine? Let the artist then consider his protest against non-art, and remember that his voice is no more than a plea or a prayer, the full realization of which would silence the need for its very self.